STEP BY STEP
PITCHES AND PROPOSALS

A WORKBOOK FOR WRITERS

Write New!
Jul Marr *August '*

by
CHIP MACGREGOR
HOLLY LORINCZ

*The Benchmark
Press*

CHIP MACGREGOR is a leader in the publishing industry, ranked on *Publisher's Marketplace* as one of the top selling literary agents in the U.S. He owns MacGregor Literary, one of the most successful agencies in the country, but he started his career almost thirty years ago. He has written over ninety published titles, worked as an agent with Alive Communications, and was a publisher with Time Warner Book Group. His current list of clients reads like a *Who's Who* of bestselling and award winning authors, and he is popular as a keynote speaker and workshop instructor at national writing conferences.

HOLLY LORINCZ is a literary agent with MacGregor Literary, and the owner of Lorincz Literary Services, an editing and publishing company that regularly works with NY Times Bestselling authors. She is also an award winning novelist, a nationally recognized speaking coach, and a long-time writing instructor.

STEP BY STEP PITCHES AND PROPOSALS
A Workbook for Writers
by Chip MacGregor and Holly Lorincz

2015 © The Benchmark Press

For more information about this book or the authors, visit
http://www.chipmacgregor.com

ISBN-10: 0996119221
ISBN-13: 978-0-9961192-2-1
EBook ISBN: 978-0-9961192-3-8

MacGregor Literary Inc.
PO Box 1316
Manzanita, OR 97130

Cover Design by
Keri Knudson, Alchemy Book Covers

Interior Design by
Holly Lorincz, Lorincz Literary Services

DEDICATED
to Marie,
with appreciation.
—Chip

to Arne Braten,
for supporting the arts.
And the artist.
—Holly

TABLE OF CONTENTS

INTRODUCTION

Your novel is professionally edited, revised, and ready to go. Your nonfiction book is researched and fleshed out, with at least three chapters written and edited. So, how do you get someone to look at your book? How do you get a publishing house to pull *your* manuscript out of Mt. Slush Pile and, then, keep reading?

Assuming you plan to traditionally publish, you will need to start querying industry professionals in order to pitch your book—which means having a formatted, proofread manuscript and an eye-catching proposal.

Query, pitch, proposal. It seems pretty simple. But you are entering into the fray, joining hordes and hordes and *hordes* of writers seeking publication. Your first, best offense is getting your foot in the door, and keeping it there, so make sure you are going about the submission process professionally. That you are able to clearly, concisely, and with evidence show the publisher why she or he absolutely needs your book.

Don't worry. We've got your back. Coming up with a pitch so you can query a living, breathing editor is daunting, but we can help. I've seen the good, the bad, and the bleed-from-the-eyes ugly. Which is why I began teaching workshops years ago and, now, why we've put together a workbook providing clear explanations, plenty of pitch, query letter, and proposal examples, as well as handy worksheets, in an easy to use reference book. By the time you finish these pages, you can stride confidently into that conference, proposal in hand, primed to face an agent or editor (and I can stop bleeding from the eyes). If your book is ready, then you'll be ready.

- Chip MacGregor

PART 1
QUERYING

QUESTIONS ANSWERED IN THIS SECTION:
What is a query?
Are you ready to query?
Who should you be querying?
How can you find agent or editor in order to actually query?

To query, in the literary business, is to go after agents and editors, to approach industry people in order to pitch your book. Your goal is to get them to read your proposal. Let me repeat that: your goal is to get them to read your *proposal.* No industry professional has the time to look out the window, much less sit down and read your unsolicited manuscript. Entice them with your pitch so they'll want to see the details, and then give them those details in a quick, industry standard proposal and, finally, walk away praying they're going to want the full manuscript. The goal isn't to move them from "I don't know you" to "Let me make an offer on your book." The goal is to move them from "I don't know you" to "Your book sounds interesting . . . I'll have a look."

If you are sending a query letter, it should be only three to four paragraphs long and contain your pitch, your writing bio, manuscript status, and comparable titles. If you are querying face-to-face during a conference, where you've signed up for appointments with editors and agents, your query will have these same elements, beginning with a verbal pitch lasting no longer than four or five minutes.

Again, there's no need to panic; we're going to walk you through this in the following sections, with plenty of details and examples regarding face-to-face pitching, query letters, and full proposals.

However, before you even consider querying, you need to make sure your latest manuscript draft is honed and polished, including a developmental edit (i.e., has your novel's plot or structural flaws been revised? In a nonfiction book, is your overall argument complete and logical?) and a final proofreading, preferably from a professional editor. If you are serious about publishing, you need to take yourself—and your manuscript—seriously.

As you begin your search for contacts, make sure you are looking for the people working in your genre or topic area. Research the agent or editor to see if he or she has dealt with projects similar to yours, or clearly has a background or interest in your topic. I cannot stress this enough: *There is nothing an agent hates more than to be queried by a writer who has not done even a cursory search of the agency's client list,* instead randomly sending in an Amish novel when the agency only handles diet and health books. And don't try to lump your book in with a genre where it doesn't belong in order to get an agent to take a look. I'm never going to be thrilled with taking the time to read what's been touted as a natural history book only to discover it's actually werewolf erotica. Pulling a fast one on an agent or editor will not get you anywhere. You might think once they start reading your masterpiece they'll be won over by your brilliance—instead, they will use your title page as a dart board, since you just stole time away from their legitimate clients.

So, how do you find contact information for these people? No doubt about it, locating current data in order to connect with an agent can be tough. Your best bet is to attend conferences where you can meet with agents and editors for those ten minute pitching appointments. Be sure to read their bios and acquisition interests before you sign up.

Your other option is to research contact information in books or on the internet. This means you are trying to find someone to whom you are going to send an unsolicited manuscript. Remember, *these people are not obligated to look at your manuscript, or even respond*, so make sure you give this one shot your best go. You should always be polite, concise, non-threatening, non-soap-boxy, confident-but-not-arrogant, and truthful.

Some places to begin your search:
- www.publishersmarketplace.com
- www.writersdigest.com
- www.pw.org
- writing or publishing blogs
- Bio pages from past conferences
- Go to libraries, bookstores, online bookstores (Books-A-Million, Powell's, Amazon), and book review sites (GoodReads, Kirkus, etc.) to find books comparable to yours. The publishing house is listed on the copyright page and, if you're lucky, the specific editor and agent will be named in the acknowledgements in the back.

As you are collecting this information, be sure to keep track of the comparable titles and publication data, which you will need for your query and for your proposal. Also, pay attention to what makes your manuscript stand out from the other books in your area.

The next sections will walk you through how to create a pitch, and how to incorporate that pitch into a face-to-face meeting, as well as a formal query letter and proposal.

PART 2
THE FACE-TO-FACE PITCH

QUESTIONS ANSWERED IN THIS SECTION:
What information should you include in your pitch?
What does a solid verbal pitch look like?

The agent slowly leans forward, and looks you in the eye. "Your idea sounds fantastic. Do you have a proposal with you?" she says.

You did it! You pitched your book to a professional—and you got her attention. So, what did you do, exactly?

Clearly, you followed my instructions. For those of you *not* in the know, your pitch is the most important part of your query, should be short and interesting, and sell *you*, the author, as much as your book (i.e., don't come across as crazy or a jerk). In *Part 3: The Query Letter*, we will show you how to pitch in a query letter, but this section focuses on how to conduct a real-time pitching appointment with professionals. Before we describe the elements you should include in a pitch, here are some general tips for face-to-face meetings:

- Only pitch one book during an appointment.
- As you're working on your pitch, write it out, whether you're going to do this face-to-face or in a letter.
- If possible, sign up for a morning time slot. They will be listening to pitches for hours each day, so try to catch them when they are fresh.
- Be on time, polite, and to the point. And get their name right.
- Dress professionally; you're meeting with the business side of the industry. They want to know you can attend meetings, meet

deadlines, conduct interviews, iron a shirt, and tie a tie. Save the flamboyant or character costumes for your book readings.

- Your documents need to be one-sided and not crumpled.

- Speak with confidence, and absolutely NEVER say something derogatory about your book or your writing ("I know it's not a piece of literature" or "I haven't been writing very long"). No need to plant seeds of doubt about your ability before they even look at your proposal.

- Speak humbly, and absolutely NEVER claim your writing is similar to or better than the literary canon greats ("My world building skills exceed that of C.S. Lewis"). No need to set yourself up as an egotistical blowhard.

- Read the body language and facial responses of the person across from you. If they are smiling or leaning forward, they are tracking what you are saying. If they are leaning back, that might mean you are sitting too close, or they are bored. Or it might mean they are tired (which they are, believe me). Make sure you change your energy at this point, like trying to sound more enthusiastic, or personable, or maybe move further away (or closer). It boils down to paying attention to your audience and reacting to their response.

- Respect their verbal response. If the person has said they aren't interested or they don't think you are ready, do not argue, or explain why they are wrong. This only makes everyone involved uncomfortable, and possibly angry. If you have time, you *can* ask a polite question, like "do you have a suggestion what might be my next step?" or "what do you think I can do to improve my manuscript?"

- Have your pitch memorized backward and forward; practice aloud until you can start to say it so it sounds somewhat natural, like you're having a friendly conversation with the agent, not like you're an alien robot fresh off the UFO. Then, when you think you are ready, practice in front of at least two or three friends, careful to make normal eye contact (don't stare but don't look around) and your volume should be neither too loud nor too mousey. Do your friends think you are coming off as a normal human, happy to have the opportunity to share your great book? Then you're probably ready. Test yourself by giving the pitch to a video camera and then assess the recording of your performance.

- Probably most important, be prepared to answer follow-up questions on comparable titles, your writing background, and especially your platform. Platforms will be discussed in-depth in *Part 4: Creating the Proposal.*

- A couple of things you can avoid if you don't want to look totally novice: You can refer to fiction manuscripts as novels or fiction books, but never as "fiction novels." Do not tell an agent or editor you've copyrighted your work, as all manuscripts are automatically considered copyrighted today, as long as you can show the written process and ownership of the idea on your computer. Do not try to make the agent or editor sign a non-disclosure form (this is common in the screenplay writing world, but not in publishing). No one is going to steal your idea. The fact is, it just doesn't really happen. If they liked your idea, they'd offer to represent you.

In the following pages you will find a breakdown of a pitch, as well as nonfiction and fiction samples, and then a worksheet for you to begin sketching out your own pitch.

PITCH ELEMENTS

Say Hello:

Start by being polite, but don't waste time. Just shake hands, sit down, introduce yourself, quickly mention why you chose them (i.e. they recently published a book in your field), and then dive in.

The Hook:

Start with one to two sentences describing the essence of your book, including the title, genre, the setting, the manuscript status, possibly a similar book or movie. Don't mention the subplots or the characters, except maybe the protagonist or antagonist.

The Need, or the Story:

Here you provide the main details in broad strokes, including the conflicts, the tone, and the take-away for the readers, in two to four sentences. Include at least one comparable title and why your book is unique and necessary. You are revealing your thesis or premise, and providing evidence that your idea is relevant and necessary for a certain population of today's readers, or that your novel has a unique spin on a well-loved thesis (e.g., good versus evil).

Your Authority:

Make sure you let them know you have written from a place of authority, that you are *the* writer for this book. If you have a platform, here is the time to mention the high points—how many followers you have on social media, if you have access to media outlets, or if you are part of an organization with a large emailing base.

Conclusion:

These people are listening to, or reading, pitches all day. Be gracious. Offer them a copy of your proposal, but don't be pushy. Sit back and ask if they have any questions. Hopefully you have five or ten minutes left to now have a discussion with the editor or agent.

If your pitch is successful, and the editor or agent asks you questions and wants to see your proposal, be prepared. Make sure you have enough copies to hand out, including samples of your writing. But be warned, the professionals rarely take copies of your material with them, as they have to travel and don't want to pack a bunch of extra stuff. Don't be offended if they give it back to you.

What you're really hoping for here is that they will give you their contact information and ask you to email your proposal. If this doesn't happen, try not to let it get you down. Go on to other appointments, considering how you can present your material more effectively, or incorporate any of the changes in your pitch or manuscript that the professional might have suggested. Go in with a positive attitude, but be prepared for the long haul.

PITCH SAMPLE

NONFICTION
Say Hello:
"Hi, it's nice to meet you, *agent's name*. My name is Heather Lawson and I am a mommy blogger. I thought you might be a good person to talk to because of your work with humorous self help books in the past year."

The Hook:
"So, my book, *You're Gonna Eat That*, is a 55,000 word self-help book for single moms who just want happy, healthy kids, five minutes alone in the bathroom—and the will-power to not throat punch the judgy-mom crowd."

The Need:
"Single moms need help, not sympathy or condescension, and certainly not time consuming recipes or scrapbooking projects. No, single moms need my time saving life hacks and guilt-free shortcuts, guidelines for using the right bit in an electric drill and going on a date with a three year old wrapped around the leg, tips for supporting the emotional and physical needs of their children in a one parent household, and a funny, empathetic voice to deliver the goods. There are great parenting books out there based on blogs, like Rachel Stafford's *Hand Free Momma*, but none are geared specifically to the single mom."

Your Authority:
"I know all about the challenges facing single moms, since I am one, but I certainly don't see myself as a victim or less capable, maybe just a bit more frayed and ready to share my hard won wisdom—which is probably why my mommy blog has been going crazy over the past year, averaging about five hundred hits a day, and called "one of the best sites for single parents" by Parenting Magazine. I also regularly write for the Huffington Post and ParentingAdventure.com, and have a BA in Communications, giving me a strong platform and the skills to market myself.

Conclusion:

"Well, anyway, I really appreciate you hearing me out. I thought you might be interested in my manuscript when I saw you published *Dreaming of Sleep*, which has a similar voice. If you *are* interested, I'd be happy to talk about my platform, writing background, the manuscript, or maybe my thoughts on the market for this book. Or, if you'd rather, I have a proposal right here; the manuscript can be completed within thirty days of signing a contract. Do you have any questions?"

PITCH SAMPLE

FICTION
Say Hello:
"Hi, it's nice to meet you, *agent's name*. My name is Heather Lawrence and I am a modern romance writer."

The Hook:
"*Judging Ben,* with a tone similar to *Northern Exposure,* is a modern romance set in a rural mill town, where the 29-year-old Judge Tina Sampson is prepared to feel isolated, but not threatened . . . or loved. The 65,000 word story is complete and professionally edited."

The Message or Story:
"The protagonist Tina has agreed to move back to Cedarville temporarily, to help her mother get back on her feet after her dad's death. She thought she could stay busy in the small town courtroom, not realizing how lonely she'd be, or how hostile the locals were to law enforcement. Which is alright, since she's in no hurry to become involved with a logger. It isn't until the tough-talking mill manager, Ben, lands in front of her bench that she considers changing her mind. Too bad he is probably guilty. And the town leaders have made it clear they expect a guilty verdict."

Your Authority:
"*Judging Ben* is my third novel, and happens to be closest to my heart, since I grew up in a rural town and know all about the ridiculous conflict between white collar and blue collar workers, as well as how to embrace true love, no matter the package. *Judging Ben* has been endorsed by Harlequin's Allison Mast, my writing mentor and author of the bestselling *Jane's Town.* My first two romances, *Take it Home (winner of the 2013 Elephant Reader prize)* and *Telling Lies,* are receiving modest sales on Amazon, both with great reviews that often compare my voice to that of Joan Aimsley and Andy Thomas."

Conclusion:

"Well, anyway, I really appreciate you hearing me out. I thought you might be interested in my title when I saw you published *Consider Me*, which has a similar voice. If you're interested, I'd be happy to talk about my platform, writing background, the manuscript, or maybe my thoughts on the market for this book. Or, if you'd rather, I have a proposal right here. Do you have any questions?"

PITCH WORKSHEET

Say Hello:

The Hook:

The Message or Story:

Your Authority:

Conclusion:

PART 3
THE QUERY LETTER

QUESTIONS ANSWERED IN THIS SECTION:
What information should you include in your query letter?
What does a query letter look like when it's done?

Pitching in person is generally preferable, since it's easier to make a connection and respond to real-time body language and questions. But emailing an actual query letter (also referred to as a pitch letter), even unsolicited, does come with benefits, like being able to provide more detailed information, showcasing your writing skills, and being able to attach a proposal and a manuscript you know will then be readily available to that agent or editor.

You've come up with a draft of your pitch in the last section. You can use that same information in a formal query letter. Before we get into the formatting and content breakdown, here are some basic tips for writing a query letter:

- Emails are more effective (and desirable) than paper versions, as the information can easily be stored, recalled, and forwarded by the editor or agent.
- We recommend querying five to ten agents and editors at a time, but be sure to track your contact information, and let them know if you sign with someone. Wait six weeks and then query a wider circle of people if you have not heard back.
- Be prepared, you may or may not receive responses, as editors and agents are not required to respond to unsolicited queries. This doesn't make them heartless, it just means there isn't

enough time in the day to get through their slushpile, much less read unsolicited emails.

- Absolutely do not send your query letter as a mass email. Address each letter individually, using specific individual and business names (spelled correctly!), tailoring the information to each editor or agent.
- If you have been referred by a mutual acquaintance, be sure to open by referencing that connection.
- If you have been endorsed by a household name or an authority in your topic area, be sure to open with that reference.
- Industry people receive dozens, sometimes hundreds, of queries a week. Their time is limited and precious. Be sure you are sending to someone who has a connection to your genre or topic.
- The subject line should be obvious, such as, "Query: historical fiction based on Lincoln's lovers" or "Query: modern romance, the story of a logger and a judge trying to find love."
- The letter should be straightforward, clear, and concise. Avoid flowery or creative language, except for maybe a clever opening sentence. Save the art for the manuscript. Like I said, we don't have time to wade through word play, we just want to know what you've got for us, if it's worth our time to open your attachments.
- If you are including statistics, titles, names, or researched facts, be sure you are accurate and truthful, and that you cite your sources.
- Be realistic about your target audience. You cannot say, "This appeals to everybody, men and women, all ages, Democrats and Republicans." That's not realistic. Editors want to know who is most likely to pull this book off the shelf. They also want to know it's an area they feel comfortable working in.
- A query letter is essentially a business letter. Remember that from your high school typing class? Follow the business letter format, even though you are sending this as an email. And if

you must for some ridiculous reason send a physical letter, be sure to use letterhead.

- Avoid sounding crazy. Or crazed. Or obsessive. Mentioning your therapist, medication, or private fantasies is not a good career move.

- Proofread. Again. Seriously. I mean it. Look for homonyms, missing words, proper punctuation, correct names, weird spacing . . . as a matter of fact, you should email this letter and your attached proposal to a friend, to make sure the formatting isn't wonky. You know how it is—the text looks perfectly fine on your screen, but shows up as a mishmash on someone else's computer screen.

- Don't forget to attach the attachments.

QUERY LETTER ELEMENTS

FIRST PARAGRAPH:
Try to introduce yourself in one to two sentences that will establish a connection. "I am writing to you because your client, Heidi Gray, offered to introduce us" or some such thing. Nothing over the top or hokey. Maybe "I am writing to you because you represented *Stuff Christians Like*, by Jon Acuff, and I feel my work will have a similar audience."

SECOND PARAGRAPH:
Introduce the Hook and Need, or Story, from your pitch. Be sure to include the conflict and what's at stake for the protagonist. If this is nonfiction, you need to describe how the information is organized (i.e., "Part One describes the history, Part Two is the problem, Part Three is the solution"), and why your take is unique and worthwhile for today's audiences.

THIRD PARAGRAPH:
Refer to your writing credentials, but keep it short and interesting and describing why you wrote this particular book, establishing yourself as the authority in the topic area. List credits, but not minor ones. Ditto endorsements or awards. We don't need to know about your personal life, or even your career, unless it's related to writing skills, your topic, or your ability to build a platform (e.g., definitely mention if you work for a morning show with a stable audience, or if you are writing about a crime and are a forensics expert). Discuss your publishing history, awards, industry connections, pertinent education or experiences, and your platform (what are some different ways you can reach people to help sell your books, like websites, professional organizations, or media you can access?).

FOURTH PARAGRAPH:
Include the word count and manuscript completion date, the target audience, and comparable titles. Also important to include is the

pertinent market information ("two out of three YA bestsellers are dystopian, similar to mine.")

FORMAL CLOSE:
Mention you are attaching your proposal and what it includes. Be thankful of their time. Make sure you've included your contact information, including a phone number and email address.

QUERY LETTER SAMPLE

NONFICTION

Date

Publishing Inc.
Attn: Janice Smith, Acquisitions
1111 North St.
New York, NY 10001

RE: Nonfiction query, 55,000-word humorous self-help

Dear Ms. Smith,

I notice you've been working with humorous self-help books lately (I really enjoyed *I'm Not Fat, I'm Phat*) and believe you may be interested in *You're Gonna Eat That*.

Based on my popular blog, *You're Gonna Eat That* is a 55,000 word self-help book for single moms who just want happy, healthy kids, five minutes alone in the bathroom—and the will-power to not throat punch the judgy-mom crowd.

You're Gonna Eat That offers help, not sympathy or condescension, and certainly not time consuming recipes or scrapbooking projects. This helpful resource is divided into three parts: House, Health, and Heart. Single moms need my time saving life hacks and guilt-free shortcuts, guidelines for using the right bit in an electric drill and go on a first date with a three year old wrapped around the leg, tips for supporting the emotional and physical needs of their children in a one parent household, and a funny, empathetic voice to deliver the goods. There are great parenting books out there based on blogs, like Rachel

Stafford's *Hands Free Momma* (Zondervan), Joselyne Decker's *Fight Like a Mother* (Amazon Digital), or Haven Kimmel's *Growing Up Zippy* (Broadway Books), but none are geared specifically to the single mom.

I know all about the challenges facing single moms, since I am one, but I certainly don't see myself as a victim or less capable, maybe just a bit more frayed and ready to share my hard won wisdom—which is probably why my mommy blog has been going crazy over the past year, averaging about five hundred hits a day (www.youregonnaeatthat.com, called "one of the best sites for single parents" by Parenting Magazine). I also regularly write for the Huffington Post and ParentingAdventure.com, maintain a social media presence, and have a BA in Communications, giving me a strong platform and the skills to market myself.

As I said, the tone and topic are based on my blog, but the book contains over 60% new material. The 55,000-word manuscript can be completed within thirty days of signing a contract. A proposal (including an overview, market analysis, fuller writing bio, endorsements, chapter-by-chapter synopsis, and sample chapters) is attached.

I'm happy to answer any questions. Thank you for your time.

Sincerely,

Heather Lawson
heather@gmail.com
(319) 319-3192

SUBJECT LINE: QUERY *You're Gonna Eat That* is a nonfiction, humorous self-help for single-moms

QUERY LETTER SAMPLE

FICTION

Date

Publishing Inc.
Attn: Janice Smith, Acquisitions
1111 North St.
New York, NY 10001

RE: Fiction query, 55,000-word humorous self-help

> *"I couldn't stop turning the pages . . . I had to add hot water to my bath three times just so I could find out what happened next in Judging Ben."*
> *- Allison Mast, NY Times Bestseller*

Dear Ms. Smith,

I am a romance writer *and* reader. I have enjoyed your line of Superromance books for years now. I believe my third novel, *Judging Ben*, would be a good fit, as it has intense romance and high stakes.

Judging Ben, with a tone similar to TV's popular *Northern Exposure,* is a modern romance set in a small rural mill town, where 29-year-old Tina Sampson, a big city judge home for a year, is prepared to feel isolated but not threatened . . . or loved. *Judging Ben* is my third novel; the 65,000-word story is complete and professionally edited.

The protagonist Tina has agreed to move back to Cedarville temporarily, to help her mother get back on her feet after her dad's death. She thought she could stay busy in the small town courtroom, not realizing how lonely she'd be, or how hostile the locals were to law enforcement. Which is alright, since she's in no hurry to become involved with a logger. It isn't until the tough-talking mill manager,

Ben, lands in front of her bench that she considers changing her mind. Too bad he is probably guilty. The town leaders have made it clear *they* expect a guilty verdict, as does whoever is sending her threatening messages.

As I've said, *Judging Ben* is my third novel, and has been endorsed by Harlequin's Allison Mast, my writing mentor and author of the bestselling *Jane's Town*. My first two romances, *Take it Home (winner of the 2013 Elephant Reader prize)* and *Telling Lies*, are self-published, receiving modest sales on Amazon, both with great reviews that often compare my voice to that of Joan Aimsley and Andy Thomas; *Judging Ben* is very similar to Aimsley's writing style in *Don't Call Me Ma'am*, which is part of the Superromance line.

I'm hoping you'll have a chance to take a look at the attached proposal which includes an overview, market analysis, awards, chapter-by-chapter synopsis, and sample chapters. There is also a developed biography, detailing my platform and ability to market myself. I'm happy to answer any questions. Thank you for your time.

Sincerely,

Heather Lawson
heather@gmail.com
(319) 319-3192

SUBJECT LINE: QUERY *Judging Ben* is a modern small town romance between a judge and a logger

QUERY LETTER WORKSHEET

FIRST PARAGRAPH:

SECOND PARAGRAPH:

QUERY LETTER WORKSHEET

THIRD PARAGRAPH:

FOURTH PARAGRAPH:

FORMAL CLOSE:

PART 4
CREATING THE PROPOSAL

QUESTIONS ANSWERED IN THIS SECTION:
Why do you need a proposal?
What kind of information should you have in a proposal?
How should you format a proposal?

Editors and agents don't have time to read every manuscript on their desktop—they need "sound bites," a way to triage their inbox. Hence, we have the proposal, which is the pertinent information offered in one, easy to skim document, sent as an email attachment with your query letter. Fiction and nonfiction proposals are slightly different, but both include these basic pieces:

- the query letter (used in the body of your email)
- title page
- nonfiction proposal overview/fiction one-sheet
- nonfiction chapter-by-chapter synopsis/fiction synopsis
- three sample chapters

Before we breakdown the elements, here are some general tips:

- Novels must be complete before you send out query letters and proposals these days. No one will read a debut author's proposal for a fiction book not yet complete and edited.
- An important note about fiction proposals: take advantage of the fact that you have *three* different ways to share your story and tantalize an editor—the hook (one to two sentences), the overview (one to two paragraphs), and the synopsis (one to two pages).

- Unlike novels, nonfiction books are generally incomplete, though fleshed out, when a proposal is submitted.
- ALWAYS read the submission specifications if they are available, and look for proposal samples on their website. Not every agency or house adheres to the basic format (though most do); some prefer a PDF over a .doc, or some want very specific headers and footers, or some want only your manuscript. We use the *Chicago Manual of Style*, by the way, as do most publishers these days (except academic presses), but there are a handful of houses that want number usage to follow AP rules, dialogue punctuation to follow the British standard, or other random idiosyncrasies.
- Word is the preferred word processing program for creating documents, but Mac's Pages is becoming popular; personally, I'd still save a Pages document as a .doc file so you know that older systems can read it. Again, your proposal is one document, with the manuscript sample included last, and your query letter used as the email message.
- Only pitch one book per proposal.
- You will find you are repeating yourself from the query letter— and that's fine. The proposal is taking a lot of the same information and breaking it into labeled sections, easy for the reader to scan.
- As in the query letter, the voice or tone of your proposal should match your book, but be careful with humor. You can spend so much time being funny or sarcastic you lose the message or offend the audience. And please, for the love of all things holy, do not send me a proposal written in the voice of the character.
- Don't use a bunch of bold, underlining, or italic formatting in your proposal, only what is necessary for subtitles or titles. Definitely do not use a crazy mix of fonts or colors. This is a professional document, not your middle school newspaper.
- The following samples do not have headers, but feel free to use a simple header on your proposal, with your last name and the title of the book centered, starting after the title page. No

matter what, make sure you have page numbers, bottom center or top right.

- A good proposal is an investment. Take your time getting the information and tone right. Remember, once you have queried an agent or publisher, you cannot query them again with this project. You will not be struck by lightning (well… probably not) but, in general, agents will only take a second look if they have specifically asked for a change *and* specifically asked you to re-email them, which is rare.

- Be confident in your delivery. Not arrogant or egotistical, but you are a writer and need to present yourself as such. If you don't define yourself as a writer, neither do we. If you don't think your book is up to snuff, neither do we. You *must* establish that your book fills a need and you're the author for the job.

- Be persistent. Send this proposal to dozens of industry professionals. In the meantime, if you do get rejection letters with feedback, carefully consider the criticism. How can you use their rejections to make your writing better? Enjoy the journey.

On the following pages, you will find a detailed list of elements for both nonfiction and fiction proposals, and then realistic sample proposals. You will also find proposal worksheets, so you can begin to develop notes for your own proposal.

Please note, your proposal does *not* have to match our samples line for line. While we have developed this particular format over more than fifteen of years working with editors and agents, this is not a format set in cement. Yes, you should include the elements we've suggested, since editors look for that stuff, but, in the end, you may want to restructure the information so it makes more sense for your particular project.

Good luck! Break a pencil!

NONFICTION PROPOSAL ELEMENTS

THE TITLE PAGE
Title:
Your title is a sales tool. In today's market, especially online, it should be salable and easy to understand. The purpose is to clearly and quickly reveal your book's basic idea or message, or pop up in a keyword search.

Subtitle:
This is an extension of the title. If your title clearly introduces the focus of the text, then the subtitle can be evocative. Or, if you do choose to use an artistic or high concept title, then you need to embed keywords into an explanatory, working subtitle.

Author name:
Use the name under which you will write the book—so use your pseudonym here, on the title page, if applicable.

Genre and word count:
List the main genre and projected word count, even if the book is not done.

Provide the contact information of who is submitting your proposal. If it is you (and not an agent), insert your name, address, phone and email address.

THE INTERNAL PAGES

TITLE INFORMATION
Author:
Provide the name under which you will be publishing. If you are using a pseudonym, be sure to include your legal name in the Biography section, as well as in your query letter.

Genre:
Here is where you state the main genre, like "Nonfiction/Health."

Tags/Keywords:
Here is where you can add the other genres you think might pertain to your book. If you have a recipe book that is also a journal, you might label the main genre as "Nonfiction/Recipe Book" but then add tags like "food journal" and "portion control."

Anticipated Word Count:
Nonfiction manuscripts are often queried mid-process, once an outline and chapter-by-chapter synopsis and a couple of chapters have been established, but you must include a projected, approximate word count.

Status:
If your manuscript isn't done, where are you at with it? Be truthful.

Completion Date:
You can give a projected date (i.e., "December 2015"), or you can say something like, "Can be completed within thirty days of signing."

Features:
Do you have maps? tables? illustrations?
How many?

CONTENT OVERVIEW

Concept:

Here you can use your Hook and Need statement from your query letter, but be sure to explain the problem you are researching and the solution you are offering ("You can escape the 9-5, live in paradise, and join the new rich"), as well as applications and practices ("I will show you how Tim went from making $40k per year working 80 hrs per week, to making $40k per month working 4 hrs per week"). This is typical for nonfiction; even a new biography of Lincoln can be evaluated in this manner, as the author is researching dimensions of Lincoln previously unexplored and telling the tale so modern audiences have a new understanding of the man. You also need to mention the target audience and why you are the one to whom we should be listening ("Readers aged 25 to 35, with recent Bachelor's degrees, will benefit from my years of experience teaching young people how to manage their money, with hundreds of success stories as templates.")

One way to approach this portion is to consider Monroe's Motivational Sequence, where you establish your authority, show the problem that requires action on the behalf of the reader, present a solution that meets the need, including an action plan, and end with a call to action.

Take-Away:

In this section, you must give the reader a reason to read this book. What will they get out of it? Something along the lines of "Readers of my biography on Lincoln will (list benefits) because the book will (list features)."

Sections:

Most nonfiction books are divided into sections or parts. Here is where you list the overall organization of your material, like "Part 1: House, Part 2: Health, Part 3: Heart."

Table of Contents:

The Table of Contents is one of your biggest sales tools, besides the cover and the title. People looking for a book on a certain topic will generally flip first to the TOC to see whether or not the book offers what they need before they decide to buy it. The TOC in today's books are almost like a subject matter outline, providing a map of the scope and sequence of the material. It makes sense to use titles that represent the topic of that chapter. For instance, the title of this chapter is "Creating the Proposal." We could have called it something else, like "Sell Yourself, Baby" but that could be interpreted in a number of ways. Some interesting ways, sure, but not in a way that helps sell this particular book.

THE MARKET

The Target Audience:

Hear me now: not everyone needs this book! No book publisher, ever, heard "everyone will want to read this" and went, "Yes! All right! We've got us a winner!" No. They want to know this genre or topic falls in their wheelhouse, that they will know what portion of the market they're targeting, what those readers look like, and how to sell to them. So, in this section, you will breakdown the most likely reader demographics, where you say, "Readers will *generally* be . . ." and describe the most likely age, gender, education level, geography, religion, etc. "Working moms in their 20s and 30s with at least a high school degree," or "College educated Christian parents with teens." You'll also want to consider the psychographics, the "why" this particular group will want this book. "Working moms in their 20s and 30s with at least a high school degree who need help making ends meet," or "College educated Christian parents with teens who are struggling to fit in to a peer group."

Affinity Groups:

Here you take a common sense approach and list some groups that would likely be interested in the topic of your book. Are there people who enjoy certain popular magazines or TV shows that might like your book? Or a professional organization that might have members who are interested? How about people who work in that field?

Competition:
You need to acknowledge the competition. What else has been written on the topic? Has it found an audience? How is your book different? Making it different is important, otherwise you are not meeting a need. Do not use this space to bash competitors, only to suggest you are filling a hole that has been left open. Negativity may be ill-received.

Comparable Titles:
You will want to list four or five titles, along with the author, publisher and year of publication, that are similar in voice, tone, topic or story. Choose books that are recognizable and have met some success, but not HUGE success. You don't want to compare yourself to the literary giants. Also, try to find books tied to the agent or publisher, if possible.

AUTHOR
The big question: Why are YOU the one to write this book? You will need to include a biography highlighting your education and experience either with writing or in the subject area, writing awards, endorsements, your platform, helpful contacts, and a description of what you will do to help market the book (e.g. social media, book readings, interviews, etc.). This is a great place to embed links to interviews you've done, or articles that have been written about you and, yes, you can include a photo of yourself, usually a professional head shot.

CHAPTER-BY-CHAPTER SYNOPSIS
A strong chapter-by-chapter synopsis is imperative. As we mentioned in the Table of Contents description, you are using the chapter titles to provide readers with an understanding of the scope and sequence of the material. In this section, you are able to provide a bit more information, two or three sentences describing the big idea or topic areas covered in each chapter. This shows agents and editors how you are building a case, or how you are scaffolding information.

THREE SAMPLE CHAPTERS

You've got roughly fifty pages to impress the agent or editor, to show your writing skills, your thought process, and your ability to pull in a reading audience—and keep them reading. I highly recommend that nonfiction, regardless the topic, has a story in the opening (we're a story based culture), that you are using an active voice versus passive, and that you break up large blocks of text with subheads (and consider using a story in each new subheaded section). And, I know this goes without saying, but . . . *proofread.*

Finally, your manuscript needs to be formatted to the industry standard, which follows *The Chicago Manual of Style,* though you will need to make sure the publisher doesn't have some quirky requirements regarding title pages, or headings, or the like.

Part 5: How to Format a Manuscript in this book has a detailed set of instructions for proper settings and formatting tips.

NONFICTION PROPOSAL SAMPLE #1

YOU'RE GONNA EAT THAT
A GUIDE TO SANITY FOR SINGLE MOMS

HEATHER LAWRENCE

Submitted by
Heather Lawrence

PO Box 1234
Portland, OR 97123
(503) 123-4567
heather@gmail.com

NON-FICTION SELF-HELP / 55,000 WORDS

NONFICTION PROPOSAL SAMPLE #1

YOU'RE GONNA EAT THAT
A GUIDE TO SANITY FOR SINGLE MOMS

TITLE INFORMATION

AUTHOR:
Heather Lawrence
GENRE:
Nonfiction / Self Help
TAGS:
Parenting, Motherhood, Humor, Mommy Blog, Single Mom
ANTICIPATED WORD COUNT:
55,000 Words
STATUS:
Seventy-five percent complete
COMPLETION DATE:
Can be completed within thirty days of signing
FEATURES:
Tables, Recipes, Photos

CONTENT OVERVIEW

CONCEPT:
Based on my popular blog, *You're Gonna Eat That* is a self-help book for single moms who just want happy, healthy kids, five minutes alone in the bathroom—and the will-power to not throat punch the judgy-mom crowd.

There is no book out there right now aimed specifically at the single mom, the woman learning to date, use tools, and change a tire in dress clothes, while working full time and caring for small children missing the other parent. Until now.

You're Gonna Eat That offers help, not sympathy or condescension, and certainly not time consuming recipes or scrapbooking projects. This helpful resource is divided into three parts: House, Health, and Heart. Single moms need my time saving life hacks and guilt-free shortcuts, guidelines for using the right bit in an electric drill and going on a first date with a three year old wrapped around the leg, tips for supporting the emotional and physical needs of their children in a one parent household, and a funny, empathetic voice to deliver the goods.

I know all about the challenges facing single moms, since I am one, but I certainly don't see myself as a victim or less capable, maybe just a bit frayed, and ready to share my hard won wisdom. Blog readers will be pleased to find the most popular posts, as well as over 60% new material in the pages.

TAKE-AWAY:
  Reader's will walk away from this book with
  - A number of useful tips for a single parent to stay organized, and perform necessary household chores quickly and efficiently
  - A number of quick and easy "life hacks" for cooking, cleaning, and household repairs
  - Tips on how to use basic tools
  - Dating tips for the newly single mom
  - A number of tips and guidelines on how to deal with different physical and emotional responses that children encounter in a one-parent household
  - A resource page for parents with struggling children
  - The knowledge that you are not alone
  - Tips on how to function within the dual-parenting crowd, or the judgy-mom crowd
  - How to negotiate through the holiday minefields
  - A smile, having been entertained by a single mom who knows how to laugh at herself and find joy in her home

SECTIONS:

Foreword
Part One: House
Part Two: Health
Part Three: Heart
Bibliography
Resources

TABLE OF CONTENTS:

A complete chapter-by-chapter synopsis is also included in this document.

THE MARKET

THE TARGET AUDIENCE:
The audience for this book will typically be a divorced or widowed female with at least a high school education, from 20 to 40 years of age, with young children in the house.

The audience for this book will typically consist of readers interested in modern parenting, organizing households, relationships, and re-inventing themselves

AFFINITY GROUPS:
- Readers of modern parenting books
- Readers of books for divorcees or widows
- Readers of *Parenting* magazines
- Readers of *Living Single* magazines
- Watchers of shows like *Oprah* or *The Gilmore Girls*

COMPETITION:
There are other books on the market by parents, including blogging parents (some are listed below), offering general life tips, from recipes to guidance on raising difficult children. However, there is no book out there right now aimed specifically at the single mom, a woman learning to date, use tools, and change a tire, while working full time and caring for small children missing the other parent.

COMPARABLE TITLES:
- Rachel Stafford's *Hands Free Momma* (Zondervan 2013)
- Joselyne Decker's *Fight Like a Mother* (Amazon 2014)
- Haven Kimmel's *Growing Up Zippy* (Broadway 2009)
- *Dreaming of Sleep* by Robert Taylor (Crown 2013)
- *Stop Making Me Laugh* by Gayle Johnson. (Prometheus Books 2014)

THE AUTHOR

BIOGRAPHY:

Heather Lawrence is a single mom with a BA in Communications from Seattle University. She is a contributor to the Huffington Post and ParentingAdventure.com, with a strong platform and the skills to market herself. Her mommy blog (www.youregonnaeatthat.com) has been going crazy over the past year, averaging about five hundred hits a day, and recently touted as "one of the best sites for single parents" by Parenting Magazine. She established the blog in 2012, and has since been invited to speak at local parenting groups, and twice been interviewed by Seattle radio stations. (To listen to a recording, please follow this link: wwx.radiointerview.com)

WRITING AWARDS:

Named "Blogger of the Year" by Hip Mama Magazine

ENDORSEMENTS:

Called "one of the best sites for single parents" by Parenting Magazine.

PLATFORM:

- Contributing member to Seattle's Parent Consortium (2400 on the emailing list)
- Writer for Huff Post and ParentingAdventure.com (thousands of readers)
- 7500 blog followers
- 3800 FaceBook followers, 4600 Twitter followers

TO SUPPORT THE BOOK, THE AUTHOR WILL DO:

- Public appearances
- Book signings
- Media interviews
- Social and Multimedia participation

CHAPTER-BY-CHAPTER SYNOPSIS

FOREWORD
An introduction by me, establishing tone and authority.
PART ONE: HOUSE
Chapter One: Organization
Explaining what you can skip, what you need to do, and what you can limit. Multiple examples of organizational tips and tools, from bathroom, to closets, to garage, to kitchen, to laundry room.
Chapter Two: Lifehacks, Shortcuts, and Tools
Detailed examples of ways to shorten or change everyday procedures, recipes and repairs, including how to change a tire, with humorous examples thrown in.
PART TWO: HEALTH
Chapter Three: Shopping and Cooking
Details on how to shop and what to shop for (both food and clothes), and time saving cooking and storage methods, kid tested.
Chapter Four: Re-Defining Exercise
Figuring out how, when, and why to fit in exercise.
PART THREE: HEART
Chapter Five: Relationships with another adult
How to find a date, how to introduce the kids, how to involve/not involve the kids
Chapter Six: Relationships with your children
Tips and suggestions on how to work with the other parent, or how to be the *only* parent; what signs of distress to watch for in the kids, and what to do about it; how to find babysitters, tutors, and counselors; conversations that should happen sooner than later; establishing rules and safe words. Medical and mental health resources.

FOREWORD

My ex-mother-in-law gave me the best piece of advice I've ever received. She was visiting my house the week I returned to work after my son was born. Glancing around, she stepped close to me and whispered, "Listen. I know my son. You're on your own with cleaning. Here's a tip: stop folding your sheets and towels. Just shove them in the closest. No one looks in there. One day, you can reclaim the space. But for now, give yourself a break where you can."

I know, I know, most of you just cringed and thought, "Who in their right mind could live that way?" Well, I could. It was difficult at first, and embarrassing when we had unexpected guests, but then I came to realize I was saving myself a good half hour every time I did laundry. My sock and underwear drawer was also a happy mess. Eventually, things calmed down, I wasn't breastfeeding and cooking at the same time, and I once again had an orderly closet and could allow guests to retrieve their own towels.

But, then, I got divorced. I moved out, and had to work more hours and take care of the dogs and kids on my own. For awhile there, I was short on time and long on chaos. Then I remembered the ol' shove it in the closet trick and, suddenly, a light came on. I did not have to follow the old rules. I could make up new ones. So began my journey to discover and implement every reasonable hack and shortcut, while maintaining the health and well-being of my fragile children, and my sometimes fragile self.

You might be a single mom, but you are not alone. You are not less capable than the parenting teams that seem to surround you at every Christmas concert or shopping trip. You can do this thing, I promise. And everyone's going to be fine. Ask for help when you can, but don't be afraid to conquer some of it by yourself, in a new way. Think outside the old box you lived in—make yourself a new one, or create a freaking circle. And here are some tools to get you started . . .

(cont...)

NONFICTION PROPOSAL WORKSHEET

TITLE INFORMATION
AUTHOR:
TITLE:
SUBTITLE:
GENRE:
TAGS:
WORD COUNT:
STATUS:
COMPLETION DATE:
FEATURES:

CONTENT OVERVIEW
CONCEPT:

TAKE-AWAY:
READER'S WILL WALK AWAY FROM THIS BOOK WITH . . .

NONFICTION PROPOSAL WORKSHEET

SECTIONS:

TABLE OF CONTENTS:

NONFICTION PROPOSAL WORKSHEET

THE MARKET

THE TARGET AUDIENCE:

AFFINITY GROUPS:

COMPARABLE TITLES:

NONFICTION PROPOSAL WORKSHEET

THE AUTHOR

BIOGRAPHY:

AWARDS:

ENDORSEMENTS:

PLATFORM:

TO SUPPORT THE BOOK, THE AUTHOR IS COMMITTED TO:

NONFICTION PROPOSAL WORKSHEET

CHAPTER-BY-CHAPTER SYNOPSIS

FICTION PROPOSAL ELEMENTS

THE TITLE PAGE
Title:
Consider keeping your title short and catchy, trying to match the mood and genre of your book. Remember, this is a working title, meaning the publisher will most likely be changing it anyway. So, yes, spend a lot of time on your title, but be prepared to let it go.

Subtitle:
Subtitles are not necessary on a novel, but some people like to use them to embed their keywords, like "Smart Mouth: A Comedy." You can also use the subtitle to show this is the first in a series, like "Target: Book One in The Assassin's Creed trilogy." But remember, you are not pitching the series right now, only the first book, which should be stand-alone.

Author name:
Use your pseudonym here, if applicable.

Genre and word count:
List the main genre and final word count.

Provide the contact information of who is submitting your proposal. If it is you (and not an agent), insert your name, address, phone, and email address.

THE ONE-SHEET
Genre:
This is critically important, yet often left off proposals. Tell me where your book fits in the market. You don't send a fantasy to an agent who only rep's historicals. Most fiction editors specialize. You can find genre descriptions online at Publishers Marketplace, Amazon, and even Wikipedia.

Tags:
If you think your book fits best in the Historical Fiction genre but also has elements of a thriller, or comedy, or romance, here is where you list the sub-genres, or "tags."

Comparable Titles:
Just like with a nonfiction proposal, you will want to list three or four titles, along with the author, publisher and year of publication, similar in voice, tone, topic or story. Choose books that are recognizable and have met some success, but not HUGE success. You don't want to compare yourself to the literary giants. Also, try to find a book tied to the agent or publisher, if possible.

Audience:
What are the demographics of your most likely reader? Describe the most target age, gender, education level, geography, religion, etc. " Secular women in their 20s and 30s with at least a high school degree, interested in fantasy books and TV programs like Once Upon a Time" or "College-educated Christian readers, 35-55, who enjoy reading stories about redemption and grace." You're not saying no one else will read your book, you're just providing a marketing stance.

Manuscript Status:
As I mentioned earlier, your novel will need to be complete, especially if you're a first-timer, or if you're changing houses. Publishers care about word count, not page count. Most fiction manuscripts are between 80,000 to 100,00 words, though some epics are as long as 120,000 words. Category romances are 55,000, historical romances 75,000.

Awards:
List any awards the book has received, but no more than three writing awards you have received as a writer. . . and don't include high school achievements, unless the award is from a recognized literary entity. You can go into more detail in the biography section, but keep it short.

Hook:

I think this is probably the second most important part of your proposal—the first is the quality of your writing. As I've said before, you have three opportunities to grab the editor's attention, three different ways to present your story, starting with a catchy, short hook (then your overview, then your synopsis). Your hook conveys your basic premise while tantalizing a would-be reader, like the teaser at a movie. Summarize your story in one sentence, and show us why it's meaningful; hooks in fiction proposals are often rhetorical questions. A hook might read, "One man went in, three came out. Cloning? Or something even worse?" You can use the same hook you used in your query letter.

Overview:

Here is where you do a quick flyover of your story. Again, you can use the same information you used in your pitch or query letter. Mention the main characters (the hero & antagonist), the core story (not the minute details), the cause (or motivation), the conflict, and the cliffhanger.

The focus will be on the early story and drawing a reader into it. This is not the synopsis, so it is not necessary to mention all the characters, the twists, or even the ending. Try to keep this a short, tight paragraph, hopefully not much longer than eight or nine sentences.

AUTHOR

Bio's are unique for novelists—the "credential" doesn't matter so much as including something about your writing background. College? Training? Mags? Papers? Short stories? Anything published anywhere? You can also include reviews of your writing, writing awards, endorsements you have or can get, your platform, helpful contacts, and a description of what you will do to help market the book (e.g. social media, book readings, interviews, etc.). This is a great place to embed links to interviews you've done, or articles written about you and, yes, you can include a photo of yourself, usually a professional head shot. Keep personal details to a minimum, but it is fine to introduce a weird or significant thing that makes you stand out, like maybe you are in the

Guinness Book of Records for the longest fingernails in the world. Who isn't interested by something like that?

SYNOPSIS

So you've got a one-sentence summary and a short description in the overview, so now you need to tell the whole story, show the publisher how the story flows from the beginning, to the middle, to the end, and that you have plenty of twists and turns along the way. Tell the story as it's laid out in the novel, including the major plot points—stating simply "this happened and then this happened and then this happened." Don't spend a lot of time on description, and tell your story in present tense. Your synopsis is a straight forward, simple re-telling; do not use a lot of word play or flowery writing. Publishers just want the information, quickly and cleanly, in only one to two pages. Capitalize the letters in the main characters' names, and use single spacing.

THREE SAMPLE CHAPTERS

You've got roughly fifty pages to impress the agent or editor, to show your writing skills, your thought process, and your ability to pull readers into your story—and keep them reading. I know this goes without saying, but . . . *proofread*. Also, your manuscript needs to be formatted to the industry standard, which follows *The Chicago Manual of Style*, though you will need to make sure the publisher doesn't have some quirky requirements regarding title pages, or headings, etc.

Part 5: How to Format a Manuscript in this book has a detailed set of instructions for proper settings and formatting tips.

JUDGING BEN

BY
HEATHER LAWRENCE

Submitted by
Heather Lawrence

PO Box 1234
Portland, OR 97123
(503) 123-4567
heather@gmail.com

FICTION / MODERN ROMANCE / 65,000 WORDS

FICTION PROPOSAL SAMPLE #1

JUDGING BEN
BY HEATHER LAWRENCE

GENRE   Fiction / Contemporary Romance

TAGS   Small Town Romance, Women's Fiction

COMP.   *Don't Call Me Ma'am,* J. Aimsley (Superromances 2014)
TITLES   *Janes Town,* Allison Mast (LoveIt Books 2013)
             Confessions of Terra Tupper, AJ Geer (LoveIt Books 2013)
             He's Mine Now, Andy Thomas (Hupper Books 2014)

AUDIENCE   Females, 25 to 45, interested in modern romance
             Females, 25 to 45, interested in high stakes romance
             Females, 25 to 45, interested in small town romance

MANUSCRIPT **Complete at 65,000 words, professionally edited**

AWARDS   3rd Prize, 2013 Soul Making Novel CompetitionWinner
             of the 2013 Elephant Reader Contest

HOOK   *Judging Ben,* with a tone similar to TV's popular *Northern
Exposure,* is a modern romance set in a small mill town, where 29-year-
old Tina Sampson—a big city judge home for a year—is prepared to
feel isolated but not threatened . . . or loved.

OVERVIEW The protagonist Tina has agreed to move back to
Cedarville temporarily, to help her mother get back on her feet after her
dad's death. She thought she could stay busy in the small town
courtroom, not realizing how lonely she'd be, or how hostile the locals
were to law enforcement. Which is alright, since she's in no hurry to
become involved with a logger. It isn't until the tough-talking mill
manager, Ben, lands in front of her bench that she considers changing
her mind. Too bad he is probably guilty. The town leaders have made it

clear they expect a guilty verdict, as does the person sending threatening letters.

BIOGRAPHY *Judging Ben* is my third novel. My first two romances, *Take it Home* (winner of the 2013 Elephant Reader prize) and *Telling Lies*, are self-published, receiving modest sales on Amazon, both with great reviews that often compare my voice to that of Joan Aimsley and Andy Thomas; *Judging Ben* is very similar to Aimsley's writing style in *Don't Call Me Ma'am*, which is part of the Superromance line.

PLATFORM   I have an established author page on Facebook (2500 likes), a Twitter following (900 followers), and access to local radio and TV talk show programs; I've done two interviews already. If published, I will happily make time for:

- Public appearances
- Book signings and other book-related events
- Media interviews
- Social and Multimedia participation
- Website tie-in

ENDORSED This book has been endorsed by Harlequin's Allison Mast, my writing mentor and author of the bestselling *Jane's Town*, who has written a blurb for the cover and offered to help promote the book upon publication.

SYLLABUS

TINA SAMPSON graduated from the small mill town of Cedarville and never looked back. She became the youngest judge to ever have a seat at the bench in Seattle . . . but then found her career put on hold when her father dies unexpectedly, leaving her mother to struggle with running the town market alone, while undergoing chemotherapy. Clearly, Tina has to step up.

The day she calls her mother to report she will be moving back for a year, she receives a follow up call from Cedarville's mayor, offering her a seat on the local bench . . . there is a big case looming, requiring a full time judge. Tina moves in to her mother's house to help cook and clean, then "cleans house" at the market, firing one lackadaisical employee and creating stern rules for the others. She isn't there to make friends; the locals didn't want to be friends with the law, anyway, mistrusting the politicians and lawyers who control their lives.

Over time, it becomes clear the locals are right to keep a distance from them. Tina becomes suspicious of town leaders, especially those involved with the big mill, the town's main source of income. The first hint there is something really wrong is when the mill manager, BEN SHARK, is charged with embezzlement, which is the case she's been hired to oversee. He pleads innocent, but his demeanor is surly and sarcastic, leaving a bad taste in Tina's mouth and the impression that he very likely could be guilty; she'd already run into him in the market twice and neither time did she find the man to be pleasant. Extremely handsome maybe, but not exactly charming, or well dressed, for that matter.

As the case progresses, however, she realizes his sharp tongue is the implement of a sharp mind, and that his guarded heart is quite attractive, as are his abs. She is drawn to a man she is supposed to have no contact with outside of the courtroom, though that seems impossible in the small town. Unfortunately, someone (probably a market employee) notices and begins sending Tina messages threatening first her career, and then her safety.

Meanwhile, Ben and Tina continue to have multiple heated exchanges, some as arguments, some as passionate embraces; it's always hard to tell what's going to happen with him in the room. It's also hard to tell if he's guilty or not, until she discovers he's covering for a loved one who is being blackmailed by the mayor. In the end, her mother's chemo is successful, the market is back on it's feet, the mayor and a handful of powerful cronies are put in jail, and Ben is free to fall into Tina's bed and stay there.

SAMPLE CHAPTERS

JUDGING BEN
BY HEATHER LAWRENCE

CHAPTER ONE

"Lady, you don't know what in the hell you are talking about." The tall, angry man tugged at his beard and glared at the robed woman behind the bench.

She sighed. *This is exactly how I pictured it. Why do I always have to be right?* Rubbing her temple briefly, she eyed the logger in front of her, still wearing his mud-clogged cork boots, probably as a sign of defiance. As if she'd care he was leaving holes in the floor of this courtroom. A courtroom she hoped to walk away from in a few months and never see again. She shouldn't have agreed to come back here in the first place.

"Look, Mr. Hall, I'm only going to remind you one more time. You must show the court respect, whether you agree with me or not. Otherwise, you're going to be spending the night in jail. Again." She held up her hand when he opened his mouth in protest. "Seriously. Shut. Up." His mouth was still open but nothing was coming out. Except the stink of hatred for "the man," even though *this* man was a woman. A young female judge in a small mill town was about as popular as a rat in an outhouse. She smirked. *This town is definitely a toilet.*

She shook the thought clear. It would hurt her mother if she knew Tina was belittling Cedarville or the people. And Tina wouldn't blame her; the town really wasn't a bad place. It was only some of the people who made it unpleasant.

"You better watch your back," The logger said in a stage whisper. He just couldn't help himself.

Watching Mr. Hall be trundled out of the courtroom by the bailiff and a guard, Tina decided it was time to call it a night.

"Mom? I'm home." Tina stepped into the old farmhouse kitchen and was immediately overwhelmed by the stink of burnt food. At least two pans emitted streams of smoke from the stovetop, apparently having boiled dry. Alarmed, Tina called out again while racing to turn off the burners and open the windows. "Mom? Mom!" (cont...)

FICTION PROPOSAL WORKSHEET

GENRE

TAGS

COMPARABLE TITLES

AUDIENCE

MANUSCRIPT STATUS

AWARDS

HOOK

OVERVIEW

FICTION PROPOSAL WORKSHEET

BIOGRAPHY

PLATFORM

ENDORSEMENTS

FICTION PROPOSAL WORKSHEET

SYNOPSIS

PART 5
FORMATTING A MANUSCRIPT

QUESTIONS ANSWERED IN THIS SECTION:
What are the industry-standard format settings for a Word document?

Agents and acquisition editors often have specific format settings they require on manuscript submissions. Sometimes these paradigms are listed within their submission requirements but, more often, the editors expect you to have ESP, assuming novice authors will magically know what they want (just like you should already know what is expected in query letters and proposals).

This is a quick and dirty list of things we know, from experience, will be helpful. Please note, these are not the same settings you use when formatting an ebook.

In the beginning there was Word, and it had settings. And it was good.

And, boy, have these settings evolved. This is not the double-spaced, stretched justification from your (technological) youth. Of course, it's best to set up your document before you begin . . . but who really does that? You usually hammer out at least forty-five pages before you realize you forgot to set chapter headings or change the font from Cambria. So, let's say you're a good chunk of the way into your masterpiece, or you're done. Just "select-all" and make the following changes to your Microsoft Word doc., which you will be sending as an email attachment. One attachment. Meaning, do NOT send the chapters as individual attachments, nor mess around with anything other than Word. Automatic death sentence. And, for the love of our dwindling carbon-sucking trees, do not send a paper version.

This is not a list set on a stone tablet. Always be sure to check for quirky requests on submission forms. For instance, there are probably still two people out there, somewhere, who prefer pdf's over .doc's, and you know there's some old guy hunched over a press, demanding 14 point Garamond font. So do what your teachers told you to do, read the instructions. If there are none to be found, here are the basic rules of thumb:

- BE CONSISTENT. Most houses prefer you follow the *Chicago Manuel of Style* rules for formatting, though academic houses have different standards. Pick one style and stick with it (i.e. consistent number usage, dialogue punctuation, indenting, titles and subtitles, etc.)

- Use 1″ margins. Word comes preset with 1.25″ margins.

- Double-space your text, including the Chapter Headings.

- Block justify the text (though titles should be centered). Avoid stretching by going into Tools and choosing to automatically hyphenate your document.

- Single Space and indent block material like letters or speeches, or, in nonfiction only, direct quotes longer than five lines.

- Indent with paragraph returns only; absolutely no tabbing and space-barring to create paragraph indents. Change the paragraph setting to a first line indent at .25 under Format Paragraph.

- No extra spaces between paragraphs if you indent paragraphs. Sometimes Word's default automatically adds the extra line, so you'll need to re-set that feature.

- Change multiple fonts to one, and it's probably best to use Times New Roman, 12 point, black. Some editors don't care about mixed fonts or sizes, but most do. And all editors hate colored, curlicued, specialty fonts for chapter headings, title pages, or, especially, the text. Seriously. All of them.

- At the end of each chapter, insert a page break. Do not tab or space down until the cursor is forced to the next page. This screams, "Hi, I've never written a book before." Unless you're

John Grisham, then it screams, "Hi, that's what my editor is for." Are you John Grisham?

- Only one space between sentences. This is a tough one for those of us who grew up with the typing teacher crying out, "The cat ran through the door (period) (space) (space)," as your clumsy fingers clacked away on the typewriter. But, now, the computer automatically adjusts stuff (my technical term for it), so editors only want one space.

- Chapter titles should be bold, and best if they are in caps and centered. You can increase the size from 12 to 14 point, but it is not necessary. You can create a setting that will automatically do this with your headings after a page break.

- Header: Times New Roman, 12 point, centered: your last name / title

- Footer: page number, bottom center, but not on the first page

- Use italics, never underline, for emphasis or titles.

Some publishing houses have even more specific requests. Knowing houses want these settings, it doesn't hurt to go ahead and apply them anyway.

- The first line of every chapter (or after an internal transition) should be flush left, with no indent.

- Transitioning within a chapter (i.e., to show a shift in point of view or time) should not have a bunch of forced spaces, instead use a centered string of bold asterisks (**********) or a centered bold line (_____), with no extra line spacing.

- All numbers used within dialogue must be spelled out, and numbers under one hundred used elsewhere should also be spelled out, according to CMOS.

- CMOS sticklers will want only the em-dash, with no spaces on either side: ebook—just.

- Sticklers will also want you to use the *Chicago* ellipse: he looked up . . . smoke. Notice it is: (space) period (space) period (space) period (space).

- Quoting/dialogue: I'm not going to get into the various dialogue punctuation rules (see the online *Chicago Manual*), but your basic dialogue, and dialogue within dialogue, should look like this (pay attention to the spacing):

> Bob turned to me, continuing his story. "And then I yelled, 'You are one ignorant fool!' "
> Jennifer interrupted him. "He said you called him a genius, that you even claimed, 'I wish I was half as smart as you.' So, which one of you is the liar?"

- Pay for a professional proofreader. If some editors or agents catch one whiff of extra lines, tabs instead of paragraph returns, mixed fonts, typos . . . well, they may send your manuscript back and ask for it to be formatted properly, but most likely they will set it aside and pick up the next ms from the huge pile in front of them.
- Most important of all, recognize you are not designing a book. You are submitting the equivalent of a very long essay or paper. The content is the focus, which is why the formatting has become standardized. Designing fancy art for the first letter in each chapter of a suspense novel is a waste of time on a manuscript.

Finally, yes, you can hire a service (there are hundreds of editorial services listed online) to create a professionally formatted document . . . but it's probably not necessary for most writers who've used Word for a while. Most of the above suggestions can be figured out, fairly intuitively, by dinking around in your menus, or using the search bar in the online *Chicago Manual* to answer style questions.

PART 6
ADDITIONAL SAMPLES

As we've said, don't feel like you have to use our proposal template word for word, or even section by section. It's most important you have the key information, that it's written clearly and concisely, and the document is professionally formatted.

The following samples are examples of successful proposals that led to publication.

Good luck on your writing journey!

FICTION PROPOSAL SAMPLE #2

[This proposal sold to Llewellyn in 2014, and was released under the title: Carved in Darkness.]

Title: *The First*

Hook: SFPD homicide inspector, Sabrina Vaughn, used to be someone else. Someone she spent fifteen years pretending didn't exist. When she spots a childhood acquaintance, she becomes certain of two things—that his appearance is no coincidence and that her past has finally caught up with her.

Genre: Thriller

Manuscript: Complete at 85,000 words

Author: Maegan Beaumont

Bio: Maegan is a native Phoenician, currently stuck in suburbia with her high school sweetheart and husband, Joe, along with their four children. She writes take-you-to-the-edge-of-your-seat thrillers, loves action movies and spending time with her family. When she isn't busy fulfilling her duties as Domestic Goddess, she is locked in her office with her computer, her coffee pot and her Rhodesian Ridgeback (and one true love) Jade.

Overview: Sabrina Vaughn is a San Francisco homicide inspector, but she used to be someone else. Fifteen years ago she was Melissa Walker, a seventeen-year-old waitress, described as "gentle as a lamb," who was abducted on her way home from work. She was raped and tortured for eighty-three days before being left for dead in a churchyard. Now she has changed her appearance and her name in the belief that it will make her safe from her abductor.

But in Texas the man who kidnapped Sabrina fifteen years ago has heard a rumor—that she's not dead. That she's living in California. And he is compelled to finish what he started.

But someone else has heard that same rumor—Michael O'Shea, a childhood acquaintance who now operates as an "enforcer" for a criminal organization. A year ago, Michael's sister was murdered, and he believes the killer is the same man that took Sabrina. Michael comes to California under the guise of offering protection, but what he really wants is to use Sabrina to lure his sister's murderer out into the open—and he won't take no for an answer.

Now Sabrina's kidnapper is on his way to finish what he started... But Sabrina is no lamb—not anymore. She's a lion, and she won't be anyone's sacrifice.

Synopsis: (Runs one page)

Sample Chapters:

THE FIRST
by Maegan Beaumont

Waiting was the worst part. The sporadic stretches of time between his

visits—when he came and hurt her—were the hardest torture to bear.

She had no idea how long she'd been in the dark. No longer . . .

(cont...)

FICTION PROPOSAL SAMPLE #3

[This novel series sold to Bethany House Publishers.]

COURTSHIPS OF LANCASTER COUNTY SERIES
BY LESLIE GOULD
The three-book, stand alone series, follows
three young Amish women through their courtships

Genre:
Amish Women's Fiction

Audience:
Women, ages 25+, interested in Amish Fiction

Manuscripts:
80,000 words each

Book 1 Overview:
"Courting Cate"
Catherine Miller is the oldest daughter of an entrepreneur in Lancaster County. She is smart and witty and has refused to court any of the young men in her district. When her father insists that her younger sister, Betsy, can't court until Cate does, the young men of the area take notice and hope that Pete, an impoverished man from Indiana, will win Cate's hand. But Cate's convinced Pete's motives are actually to win the affection of her younger sister—and ultimately the wealth of her father.

Book 2 Overview:
"Joining Julia"
Julia and Reuben live in Lancaster County, Pennsylvania and recruit the help of a bishop to repair the rift between their two families so they can marry. After their two groups of cousins end up fighting at a *rumspringa* party, Julia must choose between honoring her father and continuing to court Reuben.

Book 3 Overview:
"Minding Molly"
Two Lancaster County young couples who are courting, along with a married couple acting as chaperones, go on a camping trip in the Pocono Mountains. The unmarried couples are childhood friends but a recent misunderstanding between the two women, Molly and Helen, has caused problems. When one of the single men falls on the mountainside and breaks his leg, the Amish young people must rely on the help of strangers to rescue the injured hiker and to address the hurts and jealousies between the two women.

Inspiration:
The proposed stories are loosely inspired by the plots of Shakespeare's "The Taming of the Shrew," "Romeo and Juliet," and "A Midsummer's Night's Dream." The correlation between this series and the Shakespeare plays is subtle and tastefully done. Literary-inspired stories have proven popular through the years, and the retelling of classical stories has long been part of our literary culture.

Comparative Titles:
The Rose Trilogy, a three-book series by Beverly Lewis
Seasons of Grace, a three-book series by Beverly Lewis
Abram's Daughters, a three-book series by Beverly Lewis
Sisters of the Quilt, a three-book series by Cindy Woodsmall
Ada's House, a three-book series by Cindy Woodsmall
Brides of Webster County, a four-book series by Wanda Brunstetter
Sisters of Holmes County, a three-book series by Wanda Brunstetter
Daughters of Lancaster County, a series by Wanda Brunstetter
Kaufman Amish Bakery, a three-book series by Amy Clipston

Author Background:
Leslie Gould is the co-author, with Mindy Starns Clark, of *The Amish Midwife* (February 2011, #1 fiction CBA, March 2011 and #1 fiction ECPA, April 2011) and *The Amish Nanny* (July 2011). *The Amish Bride* will release in August of 2012. She is also the author of *Garden of*

Dreams, *Beyond the Blue* (winner of the Romantic Times Reviewers' Choice for Best Inspirational Novel, 2006), *Scrap Everything*, and seven Guideposts novels.

Leslie holds an MFA in creative writing from Portland State University and a bachelor's degree in history and communications from Judson Baptist College. She's visited Amish communities in both Pennsylvania and Indiana and has researched the Anabaptist movement extensively. She has taught fiction writing at Multnomah University as an adjunct professor, in public and private schools as a guest speaker, and at writers' conferences.

SYNOPSIS:
(Runs one page)

SAMPLE CHAPTERS

COURTING CATE

Chapter One

I snapped the reins, urging Thunder to move faster. The black thoroughbred had grown slower over the last year, which was why Daed insisted I use him. He'd heard too many reports of me racing my buggy along the back roads of Lancaster County.

"Giddy up!" I scooted to the edge of the bench.

(cont...)

FICTION PROPOSAL SAMPLE #4

[This novel sold to Simon & Schuster.]

THEN THERE WAS YOU
by Kara Isaac

Key Information
Genre: Contemporary Romance
Status: Complete
Length: 91,000 words

Hook
Can a girl running from her past and a guy chasing his future find the one thing they aren't looking for – love – in Middle Earth?

Overview
Dr. Allison Shire has been burnt by love before – and has the mounting legal bills to prove it. Jackson Gregory is only interested in one thing – rebuilding his business empire so he can save his family from financial ruin. When a tour of Middle Earth throws them together can they get beyond their shattered dreams to find the one thing they're not looking for?

Back Cover Copy
Dr. Allison Shire is in hiding. From her parents' very ugly and drawn-out public divorce, from her over-achieving older sister with the perfect life and from her gold-digging ex-husband, who left her with a mountain of debt and a broken heart. Though ex is probably technically the wrong term considering her so-called "husband" was already married the day she donned her expensive designer wedding dress and ruined her life. Living life on the road, traveling New Zealand as a luxury tour guide, allows her to keep running from the pain she can't face.

Jackson Gregory was on the cusp of making it big. Then his girlfriend left him for his biggest business competitor, taking his most guarded commercial secrets with her. With his business destroyed and the Iowa farm that has been in his family for generations facing foreclosure, he will do whatever it takes to convince his wealthy great-uncle to invest in his next scheme. Including accompanying him to the bottom of the world to spend three weeks pretending to be a die-hard *Lord of the Rings* fans.

As Jackson and Allie keep being thrown together on the tour, they find themselves falling for each other. But can they find a way beyond their regrets to take a second chance on love or will their pasts return to unravel their future?

Comparative Books
Jane Austen Ruined My Life by Beth Pattilo, Guideposts, 2010
Pride, Prejudice and Cheese Grits by Mary Jane Hathaway, Howard, 2014
Five Days in Skye by Carla Laureano, David C. Cook, 2013

Like the heroines of *Jane Austen Ruined My Life* and *Pride, Prejudice and Cheese Grits*, Allison Shire is an academic whose career has stalled – in this case after a woman shows up in her lecture and announces that she is also married to Allie's husband. Differing from these books, Allie's literary obsession is with the works of J.R.R. Tolkien, rather than Jane Austen. She funnels this obsession into her new job as a guide of *Lord of the Rings* and *The Hobbit* tours.

Similar to *Five Days in Skye*, the story takes place in a foreign setting (New Zealand) and the romance unfolds over a short period of time. However, it is the hero, Jackson, who is an American and out of his comfort zone in the setting rather than the heroine.

While the story covers themes such a loss, second chances, forgiveness, grace, and redemption, its more comedic style aligns more closely with authors like Becky Wade and Jenny B. Jones.

Audience

The market for *Then There Was You* is 16-45 year old females who enjoy a more humorous read with a strong inspirational message without being "preachy".

They are women who are currently reading inspirational authors like Susan May Warren, Rachel Hauck, Beth K. Vogt, Melissa Tagg and Becky Wade and general market authors like Katie Fforde, Cecelia Ahern, Sophie Kinsella and Sheila O'Flanagan. They want their happily ever after but also demand characters who are flawed, authentic, and struggle with real issues.

Marketing

- Promoting through social media and blog tours, including giveaways
- Local media blitz, including national New Zealand Christian radio stations *Radio Rhema* and *Life FM*
- Local bookstore events
- Online magazine and publications such as *Relevant* and *RadiantLit* including online radio shows and podcasts

Endorsers

- Katie Ganshert, Christy nominated *Wildflowers in Winter*
- Julie Lessman, multi-published award-winning author
- Melissa Tagg, author of *Made to Last* and *Here to Stay*
- Becky Wade, author of *Undeniably Yours* and *Meant To Be Mine*
- Rel Mollett of www.relzreviewz.com

Author Platform

Kara Isaac is an active contributor and reviewer at Novel Crossings (www.novelcrossing.com) and active on Twitter (@KaraIsaac), Facebook (Kara Isaac – Writer) and on Goodreads. Founding member of www.internationalchristianfictionwriters.blogspot.com, Kara is still active with a blog with the goal to promote writers either based outside of the US, or those whose writing is based in international settings. A new personal website is currently in the process of being commissioned.

About the Author

Kara Isaac turns thirty annually and lives in Wellington, New Zealand. Her obsession with books commenced at age one with *Scuffy the Tugboat* and has never waned. She started writing in 2005 when, after finding herself trapped for two weeks in Nowheresville, Australia with her laptop, she finally had time to indulge the growing chorus of people who kept telling her that she should "write a book". No one was more surprised than her when she actually did. *Then There Was You* is her fourth complete manuscript.

She currently spends her days being double-teamed by her ninja toddler and his four-month-old baby sister. In her previous life, she held a range of roles including marketing and communications, business consulting, and advisor to a number of Government Ministers. She highly recommends a diplomatic passport and being escorted by men with guns as a great way to get through LAX fast. She doesn't recommend saying the word "tourism" in a New Zealand accent as it can result in spending quality time with Homeland Security when the other person hears "terrorism".

A member of the ACFW since 2007 and a multi-contest finalist (Touched by Love, Heart of the West, Heart of the Rockies, and Lone Star), she is represented by Chip MacGregor. She writes what she knows, as real life provides such great material. Though, of course, all characters and events are entirely fictional and bear no resemblance to any person, living or dead or anything that may or may not have ever happened.

Synopsis

Dr. Allison (Allie) Shire is in hiding. From her parents' very ugly and drawn-out public divorce, from her over-achieving older sister with the perfect life and from her gold-digging ex-husband, **Derek McKendrick**, who left her with a mountain of debt and a broken heart.

Though ex is probably technically the wrong term considering her so-called "husband" was already married . . .
(cont...)

Manuscript Sample

The pathetic state of Allison Shire's current existence was perfectly summed up by the hairy, size-twelve prosthetic feet mocking her from the floor of the Mercedes. Their gaping depths taunted her in ways she didn't even have the linguistic abilities to express.

(cont...)

NONFICTION PROPOSAL SAMPLE #2

*[This proposal sold to Random House, and was released under
the title: Love Food & Live Well.]*

Love Food and Live Thin
How to Stop Sabotaging and Start Celebrating
By Chantel Hobbs

I. CONTENT

The Premise

It is an undisputed fact: Most of us will attempt to shed unwanted
pounds at some point in our lives. Here is the great news: We will have
success on a regular basis. However, the "not so good news" is that
according to the American Medical Association, nearly everyone who
loses weight will eventually fail and gain it back.

This roller coaster of weight management is a familiar ride for me. In
my past, I have been on it too many times to count. I know firsthand
the taste of sweet success—watching as the scale goes down, and the
thrill of shopping for a smaller pair of jeans. Then it would happen in a
flash; one day I would wake up and my smaller pair of jeans would no
longer zip. Next I would try the ol' "lie down on the bed and suck it in
trick." It wouldn't work and *here I go again*.

The feelings of heartbreak, embarrassment and defeat were always the
same. This self-defeating cycle of going up a few pounds and then
down a few seemed like it would never end. It only takes a few relapses
to realize it is not a good idea to give any clothes away after losing
weight. At some point, you will most likely need them again. At least
history has always proven this as a reality for me, the professional

dieter. Most scale-obsessed people have gone through life feeling tortured mentally, always questioning, "Why do I regularly sabotage all my weight-loss efforts?" Each cycle of losing and regaining ends with the familiar feelings of hopelessness and frustration. Even worse, it usually began with an "expert's" promise I had enthusiastically bought into.

All of this drama is cultivated from the innate hunger in each of us to find a sense of belonging, greater worth, and higher self-esteem. We are desperate to live up to a body image we have pressured ourselves into believing we can achieve. And yet the picture we have painted in our minds of the person we want to look like is usually not realistic in the first place. The reality is that most of us cannot be healthy and maintain the thin image of a supermodel. Having been this woman for the better part of my life, I thank God I am now free! After I proclaimed the vow to quit fad diets and trendy programs over eight years ago, I went on to design my own system and lose 200 pounds. More importantly, I refused to add to the depressing statistics of typical regain. I have kept it ALL off! Within me lives a clear mission each day: To use my own success and the achievements of others that I have had the privilege to coach along the way and share information that is groundbreaking and, even better, fully attainable for everyone. After ditching the diet, it is possible to *Love Food and Live Thin*.

Successful weight management for a lifetime can be a reality for everyone. It is no longer necessary to live in a state of fear after weight loss. The dreaded cycle of pounds packing their way back on can be stopped. This book will bring the reader to a new cycle where she stops sabotaging and starts celebrating!

Readers of *Love Food—Live Thin* will:

- Understand why most people sabotage their weight loss efforts.

- Recognize the many myths society and Hollywood have told and sold us.

- Identify how body image plays a role and define a "personal thin" that accurately fits their body type rather than taking a "one-size-fits-all" approach. This concept will teach the reader that the potential to be thin lies within everyone. To discover it, we start with the basis of the individual's body type. I define the different body types along with visual aids to help the reader identify her own.

- Know the difference between clean, neutral, and celebration food.

- Find effective suggestions to handle stressful situations instead of turning to food for fulfillment.

- Show how personal faith intertwined with an unconditional commitment will cause the reader to be more effective in every area of life, including her desire to keep the weight off.

This book will:

- Identify with the reader's pain and embarrassment of living on the roller coaster of weight management, just as I did for so many years. I will candidly reveal my struggles of losing and regaining as well as my certainty that I have won the battle. The reader will sense my empathy, but mostly she will now have hope for her future. I will share the truths I have discovered and give life-stories of others I have worked with who sabotaged their own efforts in the past, but have now broken free and learned a better way.

- Fully explain the carb craze, the difference between proteins, and the function of fat, as well expose the misconceptions about calorie counting. One example is whether it matters if you eat within a few hours of going to bed. Here I will teach 10 Rules for Living Thin and show the physiological way stress plays a role in our downfalls, as well as how to avoid this old excuse.

- Break down the 80/20 approach to eating, and share how to use it in everyday life. I will show how best to manage food choices while facing extenuating circumstances, such as traveling, attending functions, or when you forgot to plan.

- Give three circuit-training plans to rev up workouts and make them fun. The exercises will have instructions and photographs as well as full descriptions of the targeted muscle groups: upper body, lower body, and abdominal muscles.

- Offer a weekly checklist to stay on track which will address the complete person: Body, mind, and spirit.

The Overview

The manuscript is divided into five parts:

Part I: Crossing the Rubicon, Finding Your Point of No Return. With both ambition and serious commitment, Julius Caesar crossed the little stream called the Rubicon in 49 BC. While he knew this was going to cause inevitable war, he did it anyway because he knew it was time for change. This point of no return marked a pivotal time in history and ultimately from it came the Roman Empire and European culture. Because of the decision to cross the Rubicon, this land that was once divided fought and became one.

(cont...)

The Manuscript

1. Manuscript Status: Two chapters are completed (both are attached to this proposal as sample chapters).

2. Special Features: The manuscript will include photographs designed to demonstrate correct form for completing specified exercises. Charts and visual aids are going to be included to determine healthy body weight, body mass index, and give an explanation of the various body types.

3. Anticipated manuscript completion date: Approximately 4-6 months after receiving a commitment from a publisher.

II. AUTHOR: CHANTEL HOBBS

My Background

I have not only personally overcome the issue of how to lose weight and keep it off, I also coach others who have successfully done the same thing. At 29 years old and nearly 350 pounds, I was tired of feeling like a pathetic failure.

After crying out to God alone in a car, I made some life-altering decisions to change my entire life. After losing weight, I became a certified spinning instructor through Madd Dog Athletics, a personal trainer thru AFTA (American Fitness Training of Athletics), as well as a running coach with Team In Training (Branch of the Leukemia and Lymphoma Society).

I have an on-line training program on www.Chantelhobbs.com that has helped thousands of people around the world Ditch the Diet. I am also a motivational speaker and life coach with a base of active clients.

My Previous Writing

My first book, *Never Say Diet,* was released in December 2007 with Waterbrook Press (a division of Random House Publishing). In addition to the trade paper edition set for release in December 2008, I am also currently creating a journal as a derivative product for the same release date. This book will compliment *Never Say Diet* and give the reader specific guidance and accountability tracking with a spiritual component added in as well.

Personal Marketing

I have developed a cutting-edge web-site with videos and flash images that reaches thousands of people regularly who have either signed up to receive newsletters or enrolled in the online training portion of the program.

I am currently booked for speaking engagements every month through the end of 2008, including two major events with over 6,000 in attendance.

In addition, I have been asked to begin hosting a regular radio show on Reach FM out of South Florida that is broadcast throughout the entire state and will be called "Fit Fridays." I have recently been asked to do a weekly segment on Way FM. This is a
national Christian radio station.

In October of 2008, I will be hosting a BOOT CAMP with people who have signed up for a life-transforming weekend. We will market this event on my website as well as with local radio and television media.

In November 2008, I am planning to run the New York City Marathon. Having completed five full marathons, this will be my first time doing New York. I will be targeting media discussing my platform for a charity close to my heart that fights childhood obesity and is a branch of the New York City Roadrunner Organization as well.

I am also finalizing the details for a regularly scheduled appearance on a CBN show, Living the Life. At present, I have received confirmation that the producers are coordinating the number of segments they would like for me to tape in June of 2008 for future broadcast.

Last, my message is my life passion. I am compelled to aggressively market my story and brand every day. Because I have a strong attachment to the groups I am involved with as well, I regularly seek new and innovative ways to reach people.

III. THE MARKET

The Characteristics

The audience for this book includes
- anyone who has struggled to maintain their weight
- anyone who has suffered with a poor body image

The Motivation

People who are tired of feeling frustrated and confused when it comes to diets, nutrition, and exercise are ready to find freedom. Dieters everywhere want to get rid of their "fat clothes" with the assurance they will never need them again.

The Competition

I have yet to find a single book on lifetime weight management from someone who has lost a significant amount of weight, transformed into an athlete, and kept the weight off for several years while nurturing a family that includes four children.

IV. CHAPTER BY CHAPTER SYNOPSIS

(cont...)

NONFICTION PROPOSAL SAMPLE #3

[This proposal sold to Thomas Nelson, was released under the title Thunder Dog, *and spent several weeks on the New York Times Bestseller list.]*

THUNDER DOG
A 9/11 Story of Courage, Vision, and a Dog Named Roselle
by Michael Hingson

Go inside the stairwell of Tower One in THUNDER DOG as Michael Hingson and his guide dog, Roselle, fight their way down 78 flights of stairs through the blistering heat of the fires and the smell of jet fuel to survive the World Trade Center bombing. Michael's blindness didn't stop him from shocking the neighbors by riding his bicycle through the streets of Palmdale, California as a child, and on September 11 his blindness became an asset as he successfully led a group of people to safety during the worst terrorist attack ever on American soil.

I. CONTENT

A. The ten year anniversary of 9/11 is coming up . . . What's new here?

~ Ten years later, the Michael Hingson story helps to bring some closure and make sense of the events of September 11. The time is right for an extraordinary story of an unlikely hero.

~ The events of 9-11 still haunt the American imagination, especially in light of the continued threat of terrorism and the recent attempted car bombing in Times Square. Michael Hingson's story is an antidote; it's positive, redemptive, compelling, and has a happy ending. In addition, the

~ Each chapter includes life lessons learned from Michael's unique and heroic 9-11 experience, with additional material woven in related to growing up blind, working with a guide dog, his marriage to a woman in a wheelchair, and successfully functioning with a major disability.

~ THUNDER DOG is a detailed account of Michael Hingson's unique WTC survival experience. Although completely blind, Michael descended 78 stories in Tower One and along with his guide dog, Roselle, helped lead a group of people to safety. His story features a powerful perception of events based on sound, smell, touch, and his vision of what was taking place, along with his extraordinary role in helping to guide and calm others. Accounts of poignant life-and-death encounters include:

- o Roselle's extraordinary calm after the initial airplane impact. Even thought fire and debris was falling outside the windows, the guide dog's composure provided reassurance to Michael that there was no imminent danger and there was time to formulate a plan to evacuate.
- o Michael's positive and upbeat attitude as he took leadership of the descent. He even reminded everyone that "all this walking is a great way to lose weight."
- o Roselle's presence on the stairs made a huge impact on people and their chance of survival. Michael continued to praise her: "Good dog, you're doing great. Just keep going. You can do it." Michael sensed the others were listening not only to what he said but how he said it. "I had the sense that others kept going because Roselle and I did. I heard later that this was so," said Michael.
- o Encountering several victims burned beyond recognition.
- o A hysterical woman who couldn't breathe and who needed Michael and Roselle's reassurance. Without urging, Roselle nudged her hand, asking to be petted. The woman responded, even laughed a bit, and continued on.
- o Bodies falling or jumping from the upper floors, the smell of jet fuel, growing stronger, and the slipperiness of the stairs, starting on the 20th floor.
- o Emotional interactions with legions of firefighters climbing the stairs to the upper floors. "Even carrying

all their equipment they stopped to check on me and Roselle. As they passed just about every firefighter gave her an encouraging pat and she gave them kisses in return," said Michael. "Later, it occurred to me that for most of them, Roselle was the last living thing they ever touched and she gave them the last unconditional love they received."

- o Michael's cry out to God during the collapse of Tower Two: "How could you get us out of a building only to have it fall on us?"
- o After the collapse of Tower Two, a woman blinded by the debris cloud who needed Michael and Roselle to help her to safety inside the Fulton Street subway station.

~ Guide Dog Roselle maintained a calm and businesslike demeanor and exerted a positive effect on others fleeing the crash zone. Interestingly, early that morning, Roselle had cowered in terror during a thunderstorm at Michael's house. Yet she remained calm on 9-11.

~ THUNDER DOG is the right book at the right time with the right kind of hero—a humble man and his dog with a powerful and moving story highlighting hard-earned life lessons on teamwork, trust, compassion, transparency, creativity, and the human-animal bond.

~ Blind from birth, Michael has triumphed over adversity throughout his life and his survival skills and feisty can-do spirit prepared him to not only survive the World Trade Center attacks but to work with his guide dog Roselle to lead others to safety, too.

B. **Overview**:

THUNDER DOG is an inspirational guide to embracing life's challenges with principles forged in the fires of 9-11.

On September 11, 2001, Michael Hingson, blind from birth, was in his element as the regional sales manager of a data backup company

89

located in Tower One of the World Trade Center. His guide dog Roselle, a three year-old yellow Labrador retriever, was sleeping peacefully under his desk as Michael prepared for a routine training meeting later that morning. At 8:46 A.M. Michael heard a loud explosion and grabbed onto his desk as the building shuddered and bent over, tipping to the southwest for close to a minute. Michael said goodbye to his coworker and thought he was going to die. Slowly the tipping stopped and the building began to right itself, but what Michael did not yet know was that American Airlines Flight 11 had been hijacked by terrorists and crashed into his building 18 stories above. Millions of pieces of burning paper began to rain down outside the windows. The screaming started. And the stairs were the only way out.

This is the dramatic story of Michael Hingson, a blind man who, along with his guide dog Roselle, survived the terrorist attacks on the Twin Towers in a harrowing descent down 78 floors. Along the way, the Michael and Roselle team helped dozens of others in often surprising ways and were just 100 yards away when Tower Two collapsed. Now, ten years later, Michael reveals what he has learned about trust, courage, teamwork, and heroism both as a blind man, and as a survivor of the initial airplane attack, the 78-story stairwell descent, and the desperate sprint away from the collapsing tower and choking debris cloud.

THUNDER DOG is the astonishing account of a man who refuses to be called a hero, but who displayed extraordinary strength in the face of adversity long before September 11. It's also a heartwarming and inspirational guide to embracing life's challenges with principles forged in the fires of the Twin Towers.

C. Approach:

~ Stories are recounted in journalistic style, emphasizing dramatic moments and unexpected twists.

~ Unforgettable moments presented in scenes using imagery

90

reflecting the blind experience, with an emphasis on senses other than the visual.

~ Conversational. Friendly.

~ Life lessons shared from someone who's literally been through the fire.

~ Michael's humor, warmth, humility, and compassion emphasized.

~ Those who are sighted will be intrigued and learn what it's like to be blind. Those who are blind will appreciate reading something written from their perspective.

~ Roselle's role and her teamwork with Michael will be highlighted with an eye to the enduring popularity of dog stories.

D. Takeaway:

THUNDER DOG will inspire readers to:

~ Experience anew the tragedy and triumph of September 11 from the unique perspective of a blind person.

~ Celebrate the power of the human-animal bond in the partnership with his guide dog, Roselle, that saved Michael's life.

~ Appreciate the trust and teamwork that Michael and Roselle used to help leaders others to safety inside and outside the Tower.

~ Understand what it's like to navigate successfully as a blind person in a world designed for the sighted (or "light dependent people," as Michael says).

~ Be strong in the face of adversity.

~ Learn to use creativity, and risk-taking to survive in a changing world.

~ Employ creative adaptation and teambuilding partnerships for success.

~ Effectively develop and strengthen relationships by building on trust.

~ Be energized and motivated to respond to challenges with courage and positive action.

~ Build a life of joy, compassion, and service to others.

~ Embrace Michael's value statement: "We can do most anything we want to do."

~ Last line of book: "Don't let your sight get in the way of vision."

E. Endorsement:

Larry King, who has hosted Michael and Roselle on Larry King Live a total of five times, has agreed to write the foreword for the book. Video clip:
http://www.youtube.com/watch?v=8toQOVLVsDk&featured

II. MANUSCRIPT

A. Length: About 55,000 words

B. Completion: September, 2010

C. Appendices: A special one to two page note in Braille from Michael; a glossary of terms related to blindness; "Blindness, a Left Handed Dissertation," an essay by Kenneth Jernigan; For Further Reading; and, Notes.

D. Alternate titles:
Waterfall of Breaking Glass
Intelligent Disobedience
1463 Stairs

III. MARKET

Characteristics: Target readers include:

~ A general audience composed of dog owners, people with disabilities including blind people, business professionals, stay-at-home moms, and working class people who are interested in current events, compassionate, and somewhat socially aware.

~ People who are struggling in the current economy and need an inspirational book with a positive message coming out of 9-11 and delivered on the ten year anniversary of the event.

~ The target reader fits the Reader's Digest and the Larry King Live show demographic profile: 25-54+, with a median age of 45, a high school education and perhaps some college, and a median household income of $65,000.

~ People who purchase and read memoirs, dog books, self-help, and inspirational books. Business people who read motivational books.

~ Millions of readers who have seen Michael and Roselle on Regis and Kelly, the CBS Early Show, or his five appearances on Larry King Live.

~ Readers of Reader's Digest, which featured a story on Michael.

~ People who subscribe to the following human interest magazines: *Guideposts, Saturday Evening Post, AARP, Family Circle, People, National Enquirer*, and *Family Circle*.

~ Readers of dog themed magazines such as *Dog World, Dog Fancy, Dog Life, Bark, Modern Dog*, and *Cesar's Way*.

~ Blind people who read magazines such as *Matilda Ziegler Magazine for the Blind, The Braille Monitor* (the leading publication of the National Federation of the Blind), *The Braille Forum* (the monthly magazine of the American Council of the Blind), and *Dialogue* (a quarterly magazine with comprehensive information on blindness and vision loss).

~ People who enjoy adventure and human interest movies such as *The Blind Side, Marley and Me, Precious, Letters to Juliet, Robin Hood,*

Darfur, and *The Tillman Story.*

~ People who watch PBS or cable channels such as TLC, Lifetime, Hallmark, the upcoming Oprah Winfrey Network, Animal Planet, Discovery Channel, Total Living Network (TLN) and Christian Broadcasting Network (CBN).

~ Visitors to New York, especially the National September 11 Memorial & Museum, now under construction. A portion of the WTC Staircase that survived the disaster will be lowered into The Pit, with the below-ground museum built around it.

Competition

Books featuring 9-11 survivors, adventure stories, inspirational and motivational books, and dog stories. Books include *102 Minutes: The Untold Story of the Fight to Survive Inside the Twin Towers* by Jim Dwyer & Kevin Flynn (Times Books, 2005); *Let's Roll* by Lisa Beamer (Tyndale, 2002); *Three Cups of Tea* by Greg Mortenson (Viking Penguin, 2006); *Same Kind of Different as Me* by Ron Hall, Denver Moore, and Lynn Vincent (Thomas Nelson, 2008); *Lone Survivor: The Eyewitness Account of Operation Redwing and the Lost Heroes of SEAL Team 10* by Marcus Luttrell (Little Brown and Company, 2007); *Thinking in Pictures: My Life with Autism* by Temple Grandin (Vintage, 2006); *Scent of the Missing: Love and Partnership with a Search-and-Rescue Dog* by Susannah Charleson (Houghton Mifflin Harcourt, 2010); *September 11, An Oral History,* by Dean E. Murphy, (2002).

IV. THE AUTHOR

Michael Hingson

Background:

Michael Hingson's life changed dramatically on September 11, 2001 when Michael and his guide dog, Roselle, escaped from the 78th floor of Tower One in the World Trade Center moments before it collapsed.

Soon after, Michael and Roselle were thrust into the international limelight where Michael shared his unique survival story and 9-11 lessons of trust, courage, heroism, and teamwork. Michael and Roselle have become well known as representatives of the strength of the human-animal bond, and have been successful in communicating the power of that bond in countless media interviews and public presentations.

Although blind from birth, Michael has an indomitable spirit that first emerged when he began to spread his wings as a boy, first by riding a pedal car around inside the house, without assistance, after he learned to "hear" the coffee table. Then he shocked the neighbors by graduating to riding his bicycle, alone, through the streets of Palmdale, California. Michael was no stranger to discrimination. Raised with a can-do attitude by parents who refused to send him away to a blind school, Michael's father taught him to do math in his head and his mother taught Braille to his teacher so she could teach Michael. When he was a high school student, the school district refused to allow Michael to board the school bus with his guide dog. His father, who had an eighth grade education, did his own research and fought the system, eventually getting his son a seat on the school bus. Michael earned the rank of Eagle Scout in the Boy Scouts of America and flourished in school. During college at University of California at Irvine, he became an on campus radio personality, drove a car around campus at night, and even had his guide dog, Squire, stolen in a dorm prank. Michael took a master's degree in physics and is a lifetime member of the Physics Honors Society, Sigma Pi Sigma.

After graduation, Michael started work with Raymond Kurzweil, the remarkable inventor of the Kurzweil Reading Machine, the world's first omni-font optical character recognition system. In 2002 Kurzweil was inducted into the National Inventors Hall of Fame in 2002 for inventing the Kurzweil Reading Machine and Michael was fortunate enough to be in on the formative stages of the advancement of this reading machine from a prototype to a functioning product. During this time he met and married his wife, Karen, who uses a wheelchair.

Later Michael went to work for Quantum, a company that manufactured tape backup systems. Quantum occupied a suite on the 78th floor of Tower One of the World Trade Center.

On September 11, 2001, Michael and his guide dog, Roselle, had just arrived and settled in to work when American Airlines Flight 11 crashed into their building in the terrorist attack that destroyed the World Trade Center. They survived the initial impact and, after descending 78 flights of stairs, Michael and Roselle were just 100 yards away from Tower Two when it collapsed. After sharing his survival story on a slew of TV and radio programs, Michael decided it was time for a change. After a 27-year career in high tech computer sales and management, Michael joined the Guide Dogs for the Blind team in 2002 as the National Public Affairs director, sharing his 9-11 story throughout the world on behalf of the school. In June of 2008 Michael left Guide Dogs to form The Michael Hingson Group to travel the world speaking about the importance of teamwork and trust in our professional and personal lives, along with serving as a consultant for corporations and organizations that need assistance with Inclusive and Diversity training as well as adaptive technology training. Michael lives in Northern California with his wife, Karen. His retired guide dog, Roselle, who was cited in the Congressional Record and who won the AKC Award for Canine Excellence (ACE) in 2002 for her role in 9-11, is now 12 years old, retired, and likes to lie in the sun with Africa, Michael's current guide dog, and Fantasia, Africa's mother and a retired breeder dog for Guide Dogs for the Blind.

Personal Marketing:

1. Michael Hingson is a ready made and savvy media veteran who has earned a reputation as a compelling guest with a heartwarming and inspirational story.

2. Accompanied by his guide dog, Michael has established a solid national and international speaking platform and has made personal appearances to audiences averaging 15,000 people annually. Since

2002, Michael has personally reached well over 100,000 people (see attached speaking schedules for 2009 and 2010). Michael puts out a quarterly newsletter to organizational leaders, and will be actively soliciting newsletter signups prior to book publication.

3. Larry King, of *Larry King Live*, has agreed to write the foreword for Michael's book. Here's a video of Michael's 9/11/02 appearance: http://www.youtube.com/watch?v=8toQOVLVsDk

4. A compelling media guest, Michael has appeared on *Larry King Live* five times. Other television appearances include *Regis and Kelly Live*, the *CBS Early Show with Bryant Gumbel*, *John Walsh Show*, *Donahue*, and *Animal Planet*. In addition, Michael has been a guest on numerous network affiliate news broadcasts and radio shows both in the US and abroad, including Japan, New Zealand, Netherlands, and Canada.

5. Numerous print publications have featured Michael's story. Some of those include *Reader's Digest, National Enquirer* (American Media), and Time's *One Nation: American Remembers September 11, 2001*. Michael's story was also featured in *Inside 9-11: What Really Happened* by the reporters, writers, and editors of Der Spiegel magazine, and New York Times reporter Dean E. Murphy's book *September 11: An Oral History*.

6. Michael is affiliated with several national organizations for the blind that will contribute to the marketing effort by promoting Michael at their annual national conventions for book signings and talks.

- Guide Dogs for the Blind (Michael is a former employee, the Guide Dogs newsletter has a subscription list of over 60,000)
- Council of United States Dog Guide Schools
- National Federation of the Blind (Michael is a former employee and will be a keynote speaker at the national convention in Dallas this summer, with an attendance of 3,000)

- American Council of the Blind (15,000 members)

7. On July 6, 2010, Michael will serve as a keynote speaker at the national conference in Dallas for National Federation of the Blind, with an audience of 3,000 people. This audience is composed of the movers and shakers in the blind and vision impaired community. In the United States, there are 15 million people who are visually impaired, with 1.3 million legally blind.

8. Michael has a close relationship with the American Kennel Club, which awarded Roselle the AKC Award for Canine Excellence (ACE) for her role in 9-11. The AKC website, which generates 1.5 million unique users per month, will promote and offer the book for sale to dog lovers.

9. Plans are in the works for The Roselle Foundation. Michael will donate a portion of the book proceeds to help fund reading equipment for those blind people who cannot afford it.

10. Michael's website can drive e-commerce sales. The site features a blog, video, audio, and current news. Michael blogs on personal, social, and political topics. In addition, press kits and press releases will be available for download.

11. Michael has promotional videos available. Here are two samples: http://michaelhingson.com/newsite/videos/

12. Both Michael and collaborator Susy Flory are active in social media, including Facebook, LinkedIn, GoodReads, Amazon Author Blog, and Twitter.

13. Book reviews on Amazon, Borders, and Barnes & Noble by a network of friends and colleagues.

14. Potential bulk sales opportunities include corporations and educational entities on Michael's mailing list (see list below).

15. Back of the room sales: Michael is a willing and avid marketer with a 27-year career in high-tech sales and management. He will appear at bookstores for book signings in cities where he has scheduled speaking engagements, in addition to making books available wherever he speaks. A spreadsheet of recent bookings is attached. In addition, below is a partial list of Michael's engagements:

Akron Blind Center
Alabama Veterinary Medical Association
Associated Services for the Blind Louis Braille annual award Recognition Dinner
Braille Institute of America
California Association of Private Postsecondary Schools
California County Information and Systems Directors Association
California Technologies Executive Training Institute
Central Washington University
(cont...)
Yakima Lions Club

16. Michael will be available to promote this book in every appropriate way possible.

THUNDER DOG
A 9/11 Story of Courage, Vision, and a Dog Named Roselle

Table of Contents

THUNDER DOG
A 9/11 Story of Courage, Vision, and a Dog Named Roselle

Chapter Samples

Prologue.   Day of Thunder

1:30 AM on September 11, 2001:

Michael and his wife, Karen, were living in Westfield, New Jersey. A fierce thunderstorm assaulted the house and Michael was awakened by his guide dog, Roselle, a yellow Labrador Retriever. Although Roselle is an easygoing dog, thunder terrifies her and she was shivering by the bed. Michael stroked her a bit, then took her to his basement office. She immediately ducked under the desk, her favorite hiding place. Michael cranked up the stereo to help mask the sound of the thunder. When she stopped shaking, he began to work on his computer. About an hour and a half later, the storm had passed and they went back upstairs to bed.

(cont…)

NONFICTION PROPOSAL SAMPLE #4

[This proposal sold to HarperCollins, and hit numerous bestseller lists.]

A WARRIOR'S FAITH
The Ruthless Faith of a Wounded Navy SEAL
by Robert Vera

I. THE CONTENT

A. Overview:

A WARRIOR'S FAITH: *The Ruthless Faith Of A Wounded Navy Seal* is the account of a blinded Navy SEAL Ryan Job whose ruthless faith transformed his life and inspired others long after his tragic death. Many will remember Ryan as the inspiration for the New York Times #1 best selling book, *American Sniper* by former Navy SEAL Chris Kyle. A WARRIOR'S FAITH tells the untold story of why Ryan was so loved and admired by his SEAL brothers and friends.

B. Unique Selling Proposition:

If consumers in the target market purchase and read A WARRIOR'S FAITH then they will:

➢ Understand the full scope and sequence of military hero Ryan Job's tragedy, as well as his use of faith to transform himself and others.

➢ Be able to visualize the most important attitudes and guiding principals necessary to build and maintain a "ruthless faith" that will empower oneself and assist others.

Because the book will:

➢ Offer a first hand account of the bravery of Ryan Job and his SEAL team while in combat, and at home, including testimony from the men with whom he served.

➢ Provide a first hand account of Ryan's tenacious will to heal himself and others.

➢ Outline a path to strengthening one's faith.

C. Summary:

A WARRIOR'S FAITH breaks into seven parts.

Section 1: ar Ramadi, Iraq
This opening section introduces the reader to Ryan Job, a Navy SEAL, through the true story of the 2006 Battle of Ramadi. There are profound ironies about the Battle of Ramadi and Ryan Job. This section subtly begins a story of faith which is cleverly woven into an intricate fabric revealed at the end of the book.

Section 2: Wounded But Alive
This section is where readers learn that Ryan is permanently blinded. They are also introduced to Kelly, Ryan soon-to-be wife.

(cont…)

II.   The Manuscript:

1.   Manuscript status: Complete

2.   Special Features: Photos, maps

3.   Anticipated Length: 55, 000 words

III.   The Market

A.   Characteristics:

The audience for this book will have at least a high
school education, mainly males ranging from 18 to 65
years of age.

B.   Motivations:

The audience for this book is made up of those
interested in the military and military history, and people
who enjoy stories of inspiration and/or the Christian
faith.

C.   Affinity Groups:

1. Readers of other non-fiction books written about
military action and heroes.

2. Readers of the recent spate of military books
mentioning Ryan Job.

3. Readers looking for inspiration, particularly the
disabled or suffering.

4. Readers hungry for the lessons and wisdom of Christianity in a tough world.

D.   Competitive Titles:

While there are other books inspired by or mentioning Ryan Job – including #1 New York Times Best Seller *American Sniper* by Chris Kyle, and *Service: A Navy SEAL at War* by Marcus Luttrell – only A WARRIOR'S FAITH provides a complete picture of both his military heroism and his ruthless faith at home.   Laura Hillenbrand's *Unbroken* is similar in it's take on redemption and faith after war and Mitch Albom's *Tuesdays With Morrie* is highly comparable as an exploration of faith and the lessons found.

IV.   The Author

ROBERT VERA

In a leap of faith, Robert Vera traded his 20-year investment banking career to become a health and fitness entrepreneur. His mission was to "be significant to people" by inspiring change. One day he met a former Navy SEAL who was blind. The two developed a friendship that changed Robert forever.

A WARRIOR'S FAITH: THE RUTHLESS FAITH OF A WOUNDED NAVY SEAL is the author's account of how his friend, Navy SEAL Ryan Job, lived with ruthless faith, transformed his life and continues to inspires others long after his tragic death.

Ryan inspired Robert to continue his work with veterans and he helps to guide group of wounded veterans to the summit of Mt. Rainier and across the Grand Canyon.

After earning Political Science degree from Boston College, he began his professional career as a Staff Assistant to a United States Senator where he managed military and veteran affairs.

He later entered the investment banking industry where he worked for 20 years. In 2006, Robert answered a lifelong calling and founded a healthcare company. **In 2013 he was nominated as one of 50 people in the United Stated for the President's Council Community Leadership Award for delivering positive change to thousands of people through his workplace wellness programs.** Robert has served a number of non-profit including; Camp Patriot, The Pat Tillman Foundation, and Sentinels of Freedom Arizona. **Robert lives in Phoenix, Arizona and is an avid endurance athlete and a two time Ironman Triathlon Finisher.**

Recent interview Links:
http://www.cbn.com/media/player/index.aspx?s=/mp4/TJA27v1_WS

http://link.brightcove.com/services/player/bcpid49625183001?bckey=AQ~~,AAAABvZFMzE~,IXjx0MpOF0pugpuviAwD9l3_WMhvmNP7&bctid=1660506391001

http://www.camppatriot.org/video.html?Vid=7

SYNOPSIS

A WARRIOR'S FAITH
The Ruthless Faith Of A Wounded Navy Seal
by Robert Vera

This book is the account of a blind Navy SEAL Ryan Job, whose ruthless faith transformed his life and inspired others long after his tragic death. Many will remember Ryan Job as the inspiration for the New York Times #1 best selling book, *American Sniper* by former Navy SEAL Chris Kyle. A WARRIOR'S FAITH tells the untold story of how Ryan overcame blindness to climb Mt. Rainier, hunt a trophy Elk, graduate college with honors and explains why he was so loved and admired by his SEAL brothers, family and friends.

(cont...)

CHAPTER-BY-CHAPTER SYNOPSIS

Section 1: ar Ramadi, Iraq
Chapter titles in this section:
A Hedge of Protection
The Battle of Ramadi
"Sir Please Let Go"

Section Overview:
This opening section introduced the reader to the Ryan Job, a Navy SEAL through the true story of the 2006 Battle of Ramadi. There are profound ironies about the Battle of Ramadi and Ryan Job. This section subtlety begins a story of faith which is cleverly woven into an intricate fabric that is revealed at the end of the book.

(cont...)

ACKNOWLEDGEMENTS

Over the years, I've had a chance to work with dozens of wonderful authors, and each has brought his or her unique perspective to writing, book ideas, and the best ways to express them in proposals. My thanks to all of you for allowing me the opportunity to work with you over the years. I would particularly like to thank Vicki Crumpton, who did a workshop on proposals years ago that motivated me to write on this topic; James River Writers for asking me to teach this in a seminar; Amanda Luedeke, for making me look good; and Marie Prys, for being the best proposal editor ever (as well as a good friend for too many years to count). Thanks to authors Maegan Beaumont, Leslie Gould, Kara Isaac, Chantel Hobbs, Michael Hingson, and Robert Vera for the permission to share your excellent proposals. Finally, my thanks to Keri Knudsen at Alchemy Book Covers for the great design, Heidi Gray for reviewing the manuscript, and Holly for her work and creativity to get the whole schlamozzle completed.

—*Chip MacGregor*

Made in the USA
San Bernardino, CA
17 July 2016